TERRIE SANDELIN

Miniatures
in Minutes

- **24 Paper-Pieced Projects**
- **Complete Your Quilt with a Single Foundation**

C&T PUBLISHING

Publisher: Amy Marson

Creative Director: Gailen Runge

Editors: Jo Leichte and Kesel Wilson

Technical Editors: Jane Miller and Teresa Stroin

Copyeditor/Proofreader: Wordfirm Inc.

Cover Designer/Book Designer/
Design Director: Kristen Yenche

Production Coordinator: Casey Dukes

Illustrator: Tim Manibusan

Photography by Diane Pedersen and Christina Carty-Francis of C&T Publishing, Inc., unless otherwise noted

Library of Congress Cataloging-in-Publication Data

Sandelin, Terrie,

  Miniatures in minutes : 24 paper-pieced projects : complete your quilt with a single foundation / Terrie Sandelin.

    p. cm.

  Summary: "Book has 24 projects that can be made from 12 different foundations. Based on Anita Grossman Solomon's Fold and Sew method of paper piecing. Full-sized foundation patterns and patch template patterns are provided."—Provided by publisher.

  ISBN 978-1-57120-579-7 (paper trade : alk. paper)

  1. Patchwork—Patterns. 2. Miniature quilts. 3. Quilting—Patterns. I. Title.

  TT835.S2655 2009

  746.46'041—dc22

                              2008018895

Printed in China

10 9 8 7 6 5 4 3 2 1

Dedication

For my beloved Jeffrey, who has always believed I can do anything.

Acknowledgments

My deepest, heartfelt thanks to the many people who helped me in creating this book:

- To my brave pattern testers, Susan Rowland, Audrey Owens, Liz Marweg, and Norma Mill.

- To all my "quilty buddies," those Batting Beauties and Kindred Spirits who never fail to remind me that quilting is always about love and friendship first, fabric and rotary cutters second.

- To my husband, who picked up all the slack to allow me the time to write this book.

- To Laura Shotwell and everyone at The Fig Leaf, for getting me started and keeping me going.

- To Vickie Bajtelsmit, who quilted up a storm when the clock was ticking.

- To Margo Krager of reproductionfabrics.com, who shared her lovely fabrics with me.

- To the warm and wonderful family of C&T Publishing, who have helped make my dream come true.

Contents

Introduction

 Why Miniatures?

Why miniatures? Because they're so darn cute! There's something about those tiny patches and the way they feel in the hand that is the special province of miniature quilts. That's one answer. Here's another: Because not only *can* I start and finish a miniature in a timely manner, I *will*.

I know I'm not alone. When the subject of unfinished projects comes up, most quilters I know blush. For my part, the shelves in my sewing room overflowed with plastic containers containing partially completed quilts, all neatly labeled. The fact that I knew how to find any given project passed for my idea of organization. Not even for the benefit of your education or the cleansing of my soul am I going to admit how many of those containers were stuffed (and I mean *stuffed*) into my sewing room. What brought me to such a sorry pass? And, more to the point, how did miniature quilts become my salvation?

Like other quilters, my descent into project overload always began with temptation. Sometimes (it's embarrassing to admit this) I'd hit the boring part of a quilt-in-progress and lose my enthusiasm. Other times it was a new line of fabrics that I couldn't resist or the picture of a quilt that looked so pretty in the magazine. I would tell myself, unloading the new stash of fabric with one hand and

Something Blue, 12¾" × 13¾", Terrie Sandelin, 2007. Made with Pyramid Triangle foundation on the pullout, using Triangle Charm quilt instructions, page 34.

clutching a rotary cutter in the other, that this new design was destined for quick completion. Despite the evidence, which required no more than a sidelong glance toward the closet shelves, I actually believed that *this* project would be draped over the couch in a week, two at the outside. As Shakespeare said, "Lord, what fools these mortals be."

But, brothers and sisters (mostly sisters), I am a new woman—a happy quilter with finished quilts to show for herself. It's true! Miniatures have saved me from myself. For one, they satisfy

my urge to begin anew—a new design, a new color combination, a new fabric line. If it's a cold January day and I need to make a quilt alive with roses to bring me summer, I can. If I have a sudden urge to work with hot pink and neon green, I can. If my addiction to those gorgeous Japanese taupes overwhelms me, I can indulge. It takes so little time to move from start to finish with one of these miniatures, I can actually *complete* the whole quilt before my lamentably short attention span wanders off. To this I say, Amen!

Mountain Mist, 11¾″ × 11¾″, Terrie Sandelin, 2007. Made with 13-Square foundation on the pullout, using Diamond-on-a-Square quilt layout, page 42. Who can resist these beautiful Japanese taupes?

Besides, there's just something about a little quilt, isn't there? Like most quilters, I suspect, I was drawn to quilt-making because of how quilts embody our best thoughts of home and family, of love and comfort. They speak to my desire to make beautiful things and a beautiful home. When I hold a miniature quilt in my hands, I am brought back to the innocence of childhood, a little girl playing with dolls with miniature quilts to cover them. There's no getting around it—quilts speak to our hearts, and little quilts have their own language and their own stories to tell.

I've always admired miniature quilts. But the truth is, until discovering the possibilities of Anita Grossman Solomon's Fold and Sew method, I hadn't made as many tiny quilts as my admiration for them would suggest, because miniatures weren't only charming, they were *hard*. All those tiny pieces! And if I got just a wee, tiny bit off, the mismatched seams glared at me and looked wide as a mile. Talk about intimidating! Not only that, I just didn't have the patience. Actually, when it comes to traditional approaches to miniatures, I still don't—there's the honest truth.

Don't get me wrong. I love seeing those spectacular show-stopping quilts that win awards. The craftsmanship! The artistry! The color, the technique, the imagination! I stand in awe. I appreciate how these magnificent quilters continue to push the art of quilting into new realms. But I am not

one of their kind. Oh, I like to learn new techniques, and I like to play with color and design. But I have no illusions about how far I'm going. The winners at the American Quilter's Society aren't going to find me a threat. I'm your average, workaday kind of quilter. I make quilts that I love and that my family and friends appreciate. Like most quilters I know, that's enough for me.

What it took for me to come around to the joy of miniatures was discovering a technique that would allow me to achieve precision without turning myself into knots, a technique that was well within the reach of my technical abilities (competent but not extraordinary). The Fold and Sew method gave me just that.

My introduction to the concept came when I encountered Anita Grossman Solomon's *Make It Simpler* books. Her Fold and Sew method teaches how to paper-piece a 6-inch block with multiple sections all on a single foundation. Easy and precise. What wasn't to like? When it occurred to me that I could apply the concept to the whole design of miniature quilts, I became a happy camper indeed.

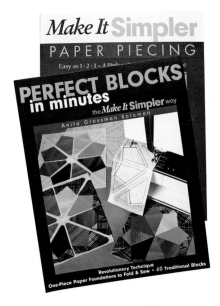

Anita Grossman Solomon's *Make It Simpler* books are available from C&T Publishing (see Resources, page 80).

Once I started making miniatures, I realized why I had so many unfinished big quilt projects. Many times, I hadn't really *wanted* to make a big quilt. Perhaps I wanted a seasonal quilt for display or to play with some wonderful fabric that had leapt out and grabbed me. I learned that a lot of times, making a miniature satisfied my creative urge, *and* I had the pleasure of a finished quilt.

My hope is that this book will appeal to quilters like me—quilters who recognize the unique charm of miniature quilts but want them to be *easier*. Once you start, you'll realize there are many answers to the question, "Why miniatures?"

- You can make one—start to finish—in a day.

- You can explore new color combinations without investing the time and money that a larger quilt requires.

- You will wow your quilting buddies.

- Little girls love them! There's just nothing like a doll quilt.

- They offer a wide range of decorating possibilities.

- They look great in seasonal displays.

- They look great on tote bags or as pillows, scrapbook covers, journal covers, and more.

- They are adaptable to any style, from Civil War reproductions to contemporary art quilts.

- They make wonderful gifts. Even non-quilters respond to the allure of these little guys.

A notebook cover provides a great opportunity to display your handiwork. Made with 13-Square foundation on the pullout, using Five Crosses quilt layout, page 44.

Create a wine bag for your favorite hostess. Made with Square-in-a-Square foundation on the pullout, using Alternating Squares quilt instructions, page 72.

So don't be intimidated by those tiny patches! Dive in. The water's just fine.

Why Fold and Sew?

Dr. Jeff's Cosmic Blocks, 11½" × 12½", Terrie Sandelin, 2007. Made with Pyramid Triangle foundation on the pullout, using Tumbling Blocks quilt layout, page 28.

Why Fold and Sew? Three words: *ease*, *precision*, and *speed*. You simply won't believe how quickly these miniatures sew up until you've made one yourself. And whereas achieving precise matches using traditional methods can be quite challenging, the Fold and Sew method makes precise sewing as easy as folding a piece of paper.

For the basic principle of sewing miniature quilts with Fold and Sew, think of a cross between strip piecing and paper piecing.

As in strip piecing, you will significantly shorten the time required to make your quilt by sewing multiple patches at once. Unlike in typical strip-piecing techniques, however, you will be sewing your patches onto a foundation.

Using nothing but the Fold and Sew technique alone, you can make a variety of miniatures, including all the Pyramid Triangle, Tumbler, and 13-Square quilt patterns. Add just a few gentle twists and turns to the basic technique and your design possibilities expand dramatically.

- *Sew and Skip* allows you to create strip quilts with long sashes and provides the basis for other pattern variations.

- *There and Back Again* mimics the traditional piecing technique of laying intersecting seams in opposing directions so the quilt top lies flatter.

- Sometimes individual blocks build from the center out, as in Courthouse Steps. *Island Joins* manipulate the joining of sections in such a way that you can strip piece these blocks while still achieving perfect seam matches with flat seams.

Remembrance, 12¼″ × 12¼″, Terrie Sandelin, 2007. Made with Duck and Ducklings foundation on the pullout. The Duck and Ducklings quilts use both the Sew and Skip and the There and Back Again techniques.

November Rain, 11¾″ × 12¾″, Terrie Sandelin, 2007. Made with Pyramid Triangle foundation on the pullout, using Diagonal Rows quilt layout, page 33. This Pyramid Triangle quilt was made with Fold and Sew alone.

Boxes, 10¼″ × 10¼″, Terrie Sandelin, 2007. Made with Courthouse Steps foundation on the pullout. Island Joins makes achieving flat intersecting seams on this Courthouse Steps mini a breeze.

I strongly recommend that even if you are attracted to some of the later quilts in the book, you begin with one of the basic Fold and Sew patterns (Pyramid Triangle, Tumbler, or 13-Square). These quilts are fast and easy and will give you a hands-on understanding of the Fold and Sew approach. The chapter Fold and Sew: A Demonstration with Pyramid Triangles, pages 19–26, contains step-by-step directions for making a Pyramid Triangle quilt, which is an excellent place to begin. Becoming completely comfortable with the Fold and Sew progression of preparing a foundation and then working with multiple patches at once will serve you well when you go on to other patterns with additional techniques.

Dawn Flight, 12¾″ × 15¼″, Terrie Sandelin, quilted by Vickie Bajtelsmit, 2007. Made with Flying Geese foundation on the pullout. Flying Geese adds on Sew and Skip to the Fold and Sew technique.

How to Use This Book

Sometimes quilt books provide helpful commentary on how difficult any given pattern may be, dividing skill levels into beginner, intermediate, and advanced—that is to say, simple, mildly challenging, and truly hairy. But, honestly, *none* of these miniature quilts are difficult to make. I do think, however, that some require more patience than others. Or, to put it another way, some require more time, because there is more work involved in making them. The There and Back Again quilts, for instance, require double-sewing the foundation, which is twice the work of the basic Fold and Sew quilts. Island Joins require more manipulation of the foundation as sections are being joined. The technique isn't at all difficult, but it is more time consuming and "fussy."

> Instead of identifying levels of difficulty, each pattern provides an estimate of how long it will take to cut the fabric, prepare the foundation, sew the foundation, and remove the paper.

In making those estimates, I presumed familiarity with the technique. Therefore, the estimates will more accurately reflect the time it will take to make your *second* Fold and Sew mini. Your first experience with a new technique will probably take you a little longer. The good news is that the Fold and Sew basics are easy to master, and you will be up to speed in no time. I also presumed a steady (though not frenetic!) work pace. Because I only estimated the time it takes to get the foundation-pieced section completed, you should allow an additional two and a half to three hours to border, quilt, and bind your miniature. It usually takes me about half an hour to add straight borders and one to two hours to quilt a miniature, depending on the complexity of the quilt design. I usually allow myself another half-hour for binding and adding a hanging sleeve, but then I machine sew my bindings. Hand stitchers should count on it taking a little longer.

> What this really adds up to is that I can, for most patterns, get from start to *finish* in less than eight hours. I just love that!

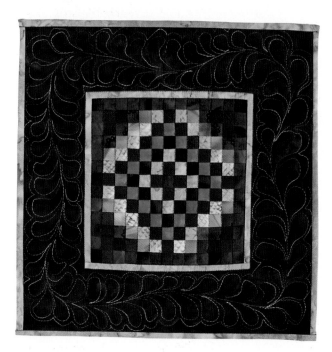

It's Too Darn Hot, 12½″ × 12½″, Terrie Sandelin, quilted by Vickie Bajtelsmit, 2007. Made with 13-Square foundation on the pullout, using Trip Around the World quilt layout, page 41. As easy as they come, the 13-Square quilts can be made start to finish in less than six hours.

Red and Black, 12″ × 12″, Terrie Sandelin, 2007. Made with Square-in-a-Square: Nine Star foundation on the pullout. The Square-in-a-Square: Nine Star is a bigger investment of time.

Once you begin, you may find, like I have, that sewing miniatures is positively addictive. Who knew?

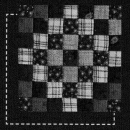

Tools and Foundations

Tools and Supplies

- **Permanent extra-fine markers in a variety of colors (red, green, blue):** You will be marking seam allowance and fabric placement guides on your foundation. Colors other than black help distinguish your marks from the printed foundation sew lines.

- **Clover Mini Iron:** This little tool neatly irons little pieces into place. It also creates less mess than a full-sized iron, which tends to smear printer/copier ink.

- **Roxanne Glue-Baste-It:** The needle on the glue bottle allows you to place small dabs of glue very accurately. Small glue dabs also make for easier paper removal.

- **Lightbox:** When using translucent vellum for your foundation paper, it is easy to see through the paper, so a lightbox is not really necessary. However, a lightbox can still make some steps in the process, such as folding foundations, easier. Likewise, with foundations other than translucent vellum, a lightbox allows you to see through the foundation material so that you can accurately mark the reverse side of the foundation.

- **Template plastic:** Some patterns require templates to ensure that your pieces are accurately sized with trimmed corners to guarantee correct fabric placement.

- **Fabric grips:** Because template plastic is slick and tends to slip (a particular challenge when dealing with such small pieces of fabric), placing fabric grips on the template helps prevent it from sliding on the fabric as you trim.

- **Sewing machine:** A straight stitch is all that is required. Needle up and needle down positioning and a knee lift for the presser foot are not essential, but they will make stops and turns easier.

- **Quilt design software:** Although quilt software isn't required, it is a useful tool. Using a quilt design program to play with color and value before you cut any fabric can really save time. Not only that, it's just plain fun. I use Electric Quilt 6 (EQ6), but other design software programs are available.

- **Miscellaneous others:** Freezer paper (to protect your ironing surface from printer/copier ink); rotary cutter, ruler and mat; transparent tape; gluestick; scissors (for fabric and for paper/plastic); thread; seam ripper (alas); and iron cleaner to help keep your mini-iron free of glue buildup.

Foundation Material

- **Translucent vellum:** I use this foundation almost exclusively. The paper is thin and see-through, creates a sharp crease when folded, and tears away easily.

- **Rinse-away:** These foundations rinse away with water. The advantage is obvious: no tearing away of all those little pieces of paper! The disadvantage, however, is that you wet your quilt. As the quilt dries and is then ironed, its shape may distort. The thicker paper can also add bulk that makes joining sections more unwieldy. Finally, because the paper is not see-through, placing patches accurately is more challenging.

- **Printer/copier paper:** I do not recommend printer or copier paper. These heavier papers add bulk and are more difficult to tear away.

Printers and Ink

- **Printer/copier ink:** When making copies, I use either a LaserJet printer or a laser print copier. I do not use inkjet printers, because I have had trouble with the ink transferring and staining fabric.

Tools for Fold and Sew quilts

Fabric Selection

One thing you'll discover with miniatures is that they can fit any style—country to contemporary, the choice is yours. What you will need to carefully consider as you choose your fabrics are *value* and *scale*. Miniature quilts offer a few challenges that their larger brothers and sisters do not.

◈ Scale and Color Contrast

Because the finished size of the patches in a miniature is so small, what might normally be considered a small-scale fabric can look quite large in a miniature. Another consideration is that a fabric with large design elements *and* high contrast will read as several different fabrics once it is placed in the quilt. For instance, this wine bottle fabric could play as either a cream, dark green, light green, or burgundy fabric, depending on where the patches fall. Unless you want a highly scattered look in your quilt, this fabric is not a good choice for a miniature.

The low-contrast red/pink/orange print provides nice contrast to the blue and white fabrics in this notebook cover.

As a general rule, tonal fabrics provide the sharpest patch definition.

Avoid large, high-contrast design elements.

This equally large-scale fabric works well, however, because the contrast is low and the colors are analogous.

Examples of tonal fabrics

Large-scale prints with low contrast are good choices.

Fussy cutting can take good advantage of a medium-to-large-scale fabric. You can choose to highlight a design feature of the fabric as is usual in fussy cutting, or, because the fabric patches are so small, you can fussy cut in "reverse"—that is, cut *around* the design element and use the background fabric.

This fabric design provides good opportunities for fussy cutting.

Fussy cutting around the larger-scale blue lines leaves a great background fabric.

Some of the same rules of fabric selection that apply to larger quilts work with miniatures as well: Variety in scale adds visual interest. In *Dargate Star*, below, the cheddar dots are quite small. The pattern of the fussy-cut squares appears large in comparison, even though in a more traditionally sized quilt block, the fabric would most likely be classified as medium scale.

Dargate Star, 11¾" × 11¾", Terrie Sandelin, 2007. Made with Square-in-a-Square foundation on the pullout, using Center Star quilt layout, page 70.

As you think about scale and contrast when selecting your fabrics, remember there is no absolute right or wrong. *What matters isn't the effect you want to create; it's that you create the effect you want.* For example, the reproduction-style Pyramid Triangle quilt *Tuesday Nights*, below, uses fabrics with medium-to-large-scale prints and relatively high contrast. The result is that some of the patches blend together and the points are muted, particularly those in the black and tan rows at the top and bottom. The Southwest version, *Desert Sand*, page 12, uses tonal fabrics, creating points that are all sharp and distinct.

Tuesday Nights, 12½" × 13½", Terrie Sandelin, 2007. Made with Pyramid Triangle foundation on the pullout, using Horizontal Rows quilt layout, page 31.

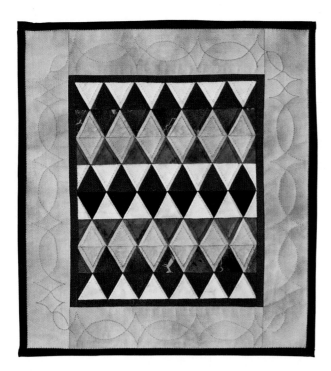

Desert Sand, 11¼″ × 12¼″, Terrie Sandelin, 2007. Made with Pyramid Triangle foundation on the pullout, using Horizontal Rows quilt layout, page 31.

Unfinished, Terrie Sandelin, 2007. Made with 13-Square foundation on the pullout, using Five Crosses quilt layout, page 44. The numerous light fabrics set against dark create too many areas of high contrast. The result? The overall pattern gets lost.

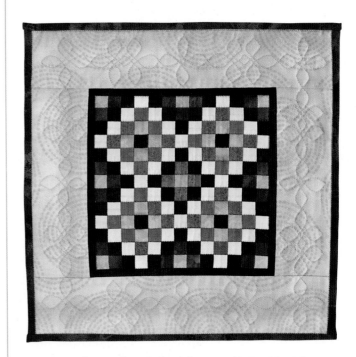

Promises, 11¾″ × 11¾″, Terrie Sandelin, 2007. Made with 13-Square foundation on the pullout, using Five Crosses quilt layout, page 44. One light fabric is often enough to provide definition in a miniature quilt.

Value Contrast in the Quilt

It is important to think about value contrast not only within a given fabric but also within the quilt as a whole. Too much value contrast and your miniature becomes visually noisy and the pattern hard to decipher. Too little contrast and the design pattern won't emerge at all.

TOO MUCH CONTRAST

In the taupe version of 13-Square—Five Crosses, above right, the contrast is too high. I actually knew this from the EQ6 mock-up I had made, but I stubbornly refused to believe what my eyes were telling me. I hoped that somehow, when I actually made the quilt, the contrast would work. It didn't. It took several weeks of looking at it on my design wall, trying to convince myself it was really just fine, before I admitted defeat, went back to the drawing board, and began again. In the taupe and salmon version, Promises, right, the white fabric provides the only high contrast, while the salmon and shades of brown provide visual interest. The result is much more harmonious.

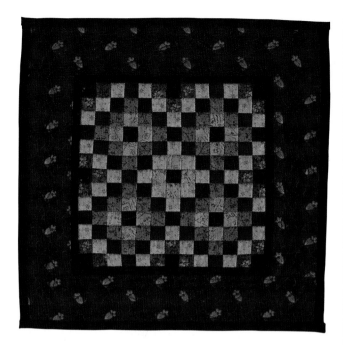

Nostalgia, 10¾" × 10¾", Terrie Sandelin, 2007. Made with 13-Square foundation on the pullout, using Five Crosses quilt layout, page 44. To provide design definition without high contrast, use mellow, shaded fabrics, which keep contrast levels quieter.

Although a single light fabric is often all that is necessary to provide pattern definition, it is possible to use more than one if you place your fabrics carefully. For instance, the Diamond-on-a-Square notepad cover, below, uses three light-colored fabrics. Because they are very close in color and value, however, they read like a single fabric with tonal variations. In addition, they are grouped together in such a way that they provide "blocks" of design definition.

Notepad cover, Terrie Sandelin, 2007. Made with 13-Square foundation on the pullout, using Diamond-on-a-Square quilt layout, page 42. Light fabrics that are similar in shading provide subtle textural interest. This 13-Square mini uses three light fabrics.

TOO LITTLE CONTRAST

Too little contrast creates much the same result as too much: a loss of design definition. Of course, this may be, on occasion, exactly the effect you desire.

Unfinished, Terrie Sandelin, 2007. Made with Tumbler foundation on the pullout, using Tumbler Charm quilt instructions, page 39. With little value contrast between many of the fabrics, no clear design emerges.

Charmed to Greet You, 13" × 13", Terrie Sandelin, 2007. Made with Tumbler foundation on the pullout, using Tumbler Charm quilt instructions, page 39. There's no absolute right or wrong. This mini's colorful blend of color is exactly what I wanted.

Saturday Mornings, 11¾" × 11¾", Terrie Sandelin, quilted by Vickie Bajtelsmit, 2007. Made with Tumbler foundation on the pullout, using Tumbler Charm quilt instructions, page 39. Using white in every other patch provides just enough design definition to allow each 1930s reproduction fabric to speak for itself.

◆ Border Fabric

Borders are your final major fabric decision. Consider them the frame that sets off the fine piecing of the interior. I always wait to select the border fabric until after I have sewn the foundation. Being able to place different fabrics against the finished foundation allows me to see how the border and foundation interact.

Just as with your previous fabric choices, you need to consider scale and contrast. For the outer border, it is often best to choose a fabric that will not "fight" with your interior. Given the small patchwork involved in a miniature, it is very easy for a busy or larger-scale fabric to overwhelm the pieced interior. Choosing a fabric that is quieter and that provides negative space around your piecework is often your best choice. A narrow inner border provides sharp definition that draws the eye; bright or dark colors provide the strongest sense of enclosure.

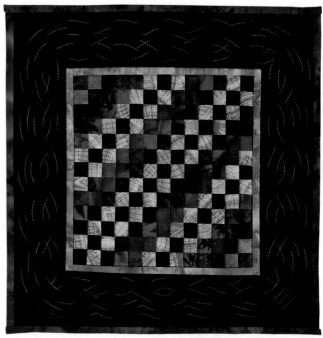

Shadowfall, 11¼" × 11¼", Terrie Sandelin, 2007. Made with 13-Square foundation on the pullout, using Diagonal Rows quilt layout, page 45.

Sometimes, however, an attention-grabbing border can be fun and will create just the effect you desire. Pictured below are two versions of the Everlasting Tree pattern. The batik version uses a quiet outer border that keeps the focus on the pieced interior. The patterned border of the pink and blue version minimizes some of the impact of the foundation-pieced inner section, but the border doesn't *quite* overwhelm the center section. The effect echoes the wonderful sense of pattern blend that some traditional, early nineteenth-century quilts achieve.

Dargate Ribbons, 11″ × 12½″, Terrie Sandelin, 2007. Made with Everlasting Tree foundation on the pullout.

Portal, 11½″ × 13″, Terrie Sandelin, 2007. Made with Everlasting Tree foundation on the pullout.

Fabric selection is always a highly personal choice. Ultimately, you have to go where *your* heart and design sense lead you. All of the previous suggestions are simply that: *suggestions*. There really are no hard-and-fast rules when it comes to quilts, be they miniature or king size. If you want a soft blend of colors, blend away. If you want eye-popping contrast, indulge. The more miniatures you make (and given how easy and quick these are, I hope you'll make many), the more you'll learn about what *you* like in a miniature quilt.

✦ Mock-Ups

The great virtue of a mock-up is that it allows you to see how the fabric choices you have made are working *before* you cut and sew. As an added benefit, it is a visual guide that allows you to check your progress as you sew, ensuring that you place your fabric pieces correctly.

- **Quilt design software:** I prefer this method. I use Electric Quilt 6. Within EQ6, I can play with variations in color, value, and fabric choice and then print out a full-color mock-up. Most quilt design programs include an extensive library of scanned fabrics. In addition, you can also download fabric scans from manufacturers' websites or scan your own fabrics and import the images into the program. I am usually satisfied with mock-ups that display fabrics that are close approximations to the ones I will actually use, as this gives me a more-than-adequate guide to the use of color and value.

EQ6 mock-up

Mittens and Bows, 12¾" × 12¾", Terrie Sandelin, 2007. Made with Duck and Ducklings foundation on the pullout.

- **Fabric:** Enlarge the quilt layout diagram by the suggested percentage to match the size of the finished foundation. Then, glue patches that are cut to their *finished* size onto a copy of the quilt layout diagram for your specific project. This method allows you to see exactly what your finished top will look like. The bad news, however, is that this method is quite time-consuming and uses up fabric.

Quilt Layout Diagrams and Fabric Guides

The quilt layout diagrams provide a letter guide to fabric placement on your foundation. You will transfer the letters from the layout diagram to the foundation, guaranteeing accurate patch placement.

Using Quilt Layout Diagrams

The quilt layout diagrams are designed to give you maximum flexibility in making your own fabric choices. Although the picture of a quilt may show the same fabric being used more than once (for instance, in more than one round of a Trip Around the World quilt), the quilt layout diagram will assign *each* repeated design element a different letter. This makes it easy for you to choose whether to repeat fabrics and where to repeat fabrics if you choose.

2	B	C	D	E	F	G	H	G	F	E	D	C	B
3	C	D	E	F	G	H	I	H	G	F	E	D	C
4	D	E	F	G	H	I	J	I	H	G	F	E	D
5	E	F	G	H	I	J	K	J	I	H	G	F	E
6	F	G	H	I	J	K	L	K	J	I	H	G	F
7	G	H	I	J	K	L	M	L	K	J	I	H	G
8	F	G	H	I	J	K	L	K	J	I	H	G	F
9	E	F	G	H	I	J	K	J	I	H	G	F	E
10	D	E	F	G	H	I	J	I	H	G	F	E	D
11	C	D	E	F	G	H	I	H	G	F	E	D	C
12	B	C	D	E	F	G	H	G	F	E	D	C	B
13	A	B	C	D	E	F	G	F	E	D	C	B	A

Quilt layout diagram for the 13-Square foundation—Trip Around the World variation, page 41: Quilt layout diagrams assign a different letter to *each* repeating element.

You have two options for transferring the letters from the quilt layout diagram to the foundation. The diagram can be used as a reference for marking letters on the foundation or be enlarged and placed under the foundation for tracing. Each diagram comes with an enlargement percentage to make it the same size as its corresponding foundation.

Kyoto Dreams, 11¼" × 11¼", Terrie Sandelin, quilted by Vickie Bajtelsmit, 2007. Made with 13-Square foundation on the pullout, using Trip Around the World quilt layout, page 41. This quilt does not repeat any fabrics in the rounds.

Made with 13-Square foundation on the pullout, using Trip Around the World quilt layout, page 41. The Trip Around the World on this tote bag repeats several fabrics.

Fabric Guides

To make a fabric guide, simply glue scraps of fabric to a piece of paper and write the letter to which the fabric corresponds on the quilt layout diagram. Stack your patches on the fabric guide so that you will always have the correct patch easily on hand as you sew.

When you repeat fabrics, you have two options for laying out your fabric guide. You can glue a separate scrap of fabric for each letter of the design, thereby repeating scraps of the same fabric, or you can glue each fabric only once and list all the relevant letters beside it. I have found it easiest to glue a separate scrap of fabric for each letter when there are only a couple of repeated letters and to write multiple letters by a single fabric scrap when there are numerous repeats of a given fabric.

This fabric guide lists letters separately, even though B/Q, K/O, and E/J/N repeat the same fabrics.

Because there are so many repeats of individual fabrics, this fabric guide lists all repeats by a single scrap of fabric.

Using Quilt Layout Diagrams to Calculate Cutting and Patch Requirements

The quilt layout diagrams are specifically designed to allow you the greatest flexibility in creating your own design. While each project lists cutting directions for the project as shown, you can use the Cutting Instructions listed below each layout diagram to calculate cutting information for any variation you choose.

> Begin by deciding where you want to place any given fabric. List the corresponding letters indicated on the quilt layout diagram. Then add up the number of patches required for each selected letter. To determine your strip length, multiply the resulting number by the patch size given with the pattern. For triangle patches, remember that a single square will give you two triangles.

For example, in *Mittens and Bows*, page 16, the triangle patches D, F, J, and L are red (see Duck and Ducklings quilt layout diagram, page 61). The quilt layout diagram shows that you need four triangle patches for each of these letters. Multiply 4 (the number of triangle patches needed for each letter) by 4 (the number of letters that use the red fabric) and you get 16. Thus, you'll need sixteen red triangle patches.

The triangles are cut from squares. Each square gives you two triangles, so eight squares will give you sixteen triangles. Multiply 8 by 1⅝" (the size of the square) and you get 13". Cut a strip 1⅝" × 13" (or a little longer to allow wiggle room for minor cutting adjustments). Then crosscut into eight squares. Cut the squares in half along the diagonal for a total of sixteen triangles.

Desert Medallion, 11½″ × 12½″, Terrie Sandelin, 2007. Made with Pyramid Triangle foundation on the pullout, using Medallion quilt layout, page 32.

Pyramid Triangle quilts illustrate the essentials of the Fold and Sew method. A demonstration of one of these quilts will provide you with the basic technique that will be used with all the other quilt patterns in this book. Variations and additions to the technique (Sew and Skip, There and Back Again, Island Joins) will be demonstrated later.

> As with traditional paper piecing, you will place your fabric on the nonprinted side of the foundation and sew on the printed side.

Preparing the Foundation

JOINING THE FOUNDATION PIECES

> Many of the foundations are larger than one page. You will need to join the pages before sewing.

1. Copy the main portion of the foundation. The top, bottom, and sides should have either a ¼″ outer seam allowance or a foundation join line. Trim ¼″ beyond the foundation join line to allow for overlap when joining. Copy the remainder of the foundation. Trim ¼″ beyond the foundation join line for overlap. *The foundation for Square-in-a-Square: Nine Star will require four pieces to be joined together on the foundation join lines; all others will have only two pieces.*

2. Place the page with the main portion of the foundation *printed side up* on a lightbox. Use a gluestick to draw a line of glue along the edge of the page with the foundation join line. Overlay the next page, printed side up, on top of the first. Use the seamlines and the foundation join lines to create an exact alignment. Tape the pages together, placing the tape on the *printed* side of the foundation.

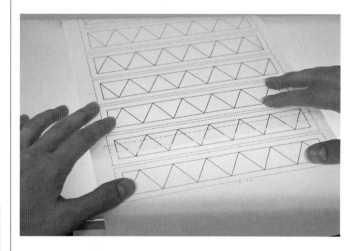

Joining foundation sections

> **tip**
>
> *Avoid having the tape cover the gap between the printed seam allowances. Tape does not hold as crisp a fold as paper. A clean, sharp fold will be important later.*

FOLDING THE FOUNDATION

1. Place the foundation page *printed side down* on a lightbox.

2. Fold the paper up and over so that two adjoining seamlines line up *exactly*. Crease; be sure that your crease lines are crisp and strong. The fold should be in the middle gap between the printed seam allowances.

Crease foundation between adjacent seamlines.

> ## tip
> *As you fold the paper, the printed side should be to the outside.*

3. Open the paper.

4. Continue to fold and crease the paper so that there is a crease between *all* rows. *Exact* alignment of the seamlines and crisp folds will create perfect matches on your points.

MARKING THE FOUNDATION

All marking should be done with permanent ink markers on the nonprinted side (i.e., the side on which you will place the fabric). Depending on the foundation material you have chosen, you may need to use a lightbox to see the seamlines on the printed side of the paper.

1. With a red extra-fine permanent marker, write "fabric side" at the top of the page on the nonprinted side of the foundation.

> ## why do this?
> *This first step isn't really necessary. However, with translucent paper, this marking helps keep you oriented as to which side of the foundation you are working on at any given time. The fabric side is the **only** side you should ever write on, and it is, of course, the side on which you will place your fabric.*

2. On the fabric side of the foundation, number the rows in the margin.

3. On the fabric side of the foundation, draw the inner diagonal seam allowances. Begin with the first patch in the upper-left corner. Align your ruler at the ¼" mark on the diagonal seamline. (The translucent paper makes it easy to see the printed lines on the reverse side of the foundation.) With the red permanent pen, draw a diagonal line to mark the edge of the seam allowance. Continue across the row, marking *every other* diagonal seamline. Repeat for each row.

> ## why do this?
> *Because your patches might shift a little during sewing, it is possible that the edge of your fabric will no longer provide an accurate guide for patch placement. Using the drawn seam allowance as your guide ensures accuracy.*

Mark seam allowances on foundation.

> ## tip: fabric placement
> *Marking on the foundation which fabric should occupy each patch will make it easy to accurately place your fabric.*

4. The quilt layout diagram indicates fabric placement. Place your foundation, printed side down, next to the quilt layout diagram. Match the numbered rows and use a blue or green extra-fine permanent marker to transcribe the letter from the layout diagram onto the matching foundation patch. Remember: Write only on the nonprinted/fabric side of the foundation. Place the letter in the far-right corner of the patch outline to prevent the letter from being covered by the previous patch's seam allowance.

> Note: Each quilt layout diagram can be enlarged and placed under the foundation so you can trace the fabric letters onto the foundation. An enlargement percentage is included with each diagram.

5. After folding and marking your foundation, you are ready to sew.

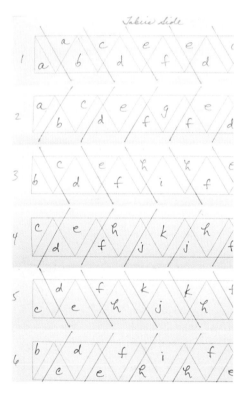

Marked foundation

> **tip**
> *Using different-colored inks makes for quicker and easier reading of the foundation as you sew.*

Cutting the Fabric

1. Trace the patch template for the project, found on the pullout, onto template plastic and cut it out.

2. Place fabric grips on the template to help prevent it from sliding on the fabric.

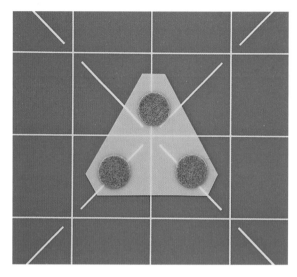

Place fabric grips on underside of template.

3. Cut fabric strips and rectangles as indicated in the Cutting Instructions for your selected project. The number of patches listed under Cutting Instructions equals the number of rectangles needed.

4. Place your template on the rectangles and trim. You can layer 4–5 rectangles at a time to cut multiple patches at once.

Use template to cut patches.

5. Create a fabric guide to match the letters on the quilt layout diagram by gluing scraps of fabric onto a sheet of paper.

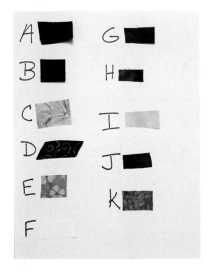

Completed fabric guide

Sewing the Foundation

STITCHING ROWS

1. Shorten your stitch length. You want stitches as small as possible while still leaving room for a seam ripper to work (on occasion, patches may fold over as you sew and will need to be removed and resewn). I set the stitch length on my machine between 1.5mm and 2mm.

2. Use Roxanne Glue-Baste-It to dab small dots of glue on the *fabric* side of the foundation. Place the dots *within the seam allowance* of the first vertical line of patches, as illustrated by the green dots in the photograph. Dab glue on *all* of the first set of patches at once—top to bottom. To avoid gumming up your sewing machine needle, be sure to place the dabs of glue so they are not directly over a seamline.

why not use a gluestick?

The needle on the bottle of Roxanne Glue-Baste-It allows you to place small dabs of glue precisely where you want them. A gluestick uses more glue, stretches the fabric, and makes it more difficult to remove the fabric from the foundation.

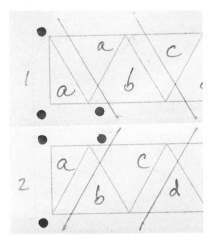

Squeeze small dabs of glue on foundation (green dots indicate glue placement).

3. Use the letters on your foundation and your fabric guide to select your fabric. Place each patch in the first set (first column) *right side up*, using the seam allowance markings as a guide. Line up the right side of the patch with the red diagonal line and the top and bottom of the patch with the printed dashed horizontal lines. (Don't worry if the fabric extends beyond the seam allowance on the left border. This will be trimmed later.)

4. Repeat Step 3 for all of the first patch set, placing them right side up from top to bottom.

First set of patches in place

5. Dab small dots of glue within the seam allowance of the first set of patches. Place dabs of glue on all of the patches at once, top to bottom. The glue dabs do not need to be very large; this is a case where more is not necessarily better!

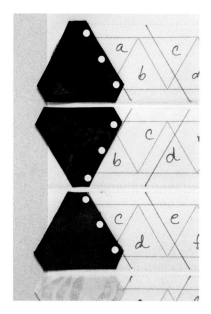

Dab glue in seam allowances (green dots indicate glue placement).

6. Place the second set of patches *right side down* on top of the first set.

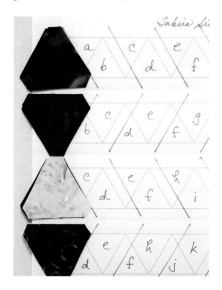

Place second set of patches.

7. Flip over the foundation and sew the diagonal seamline on the *printed* side of the foundation. Sew the entire seamline from the top of the foundation to the bottom. Sew through the seam allowances and pivot at the folded crease line between the rows.

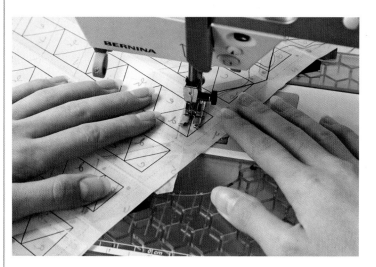

Stitch on printed side, zigzagging from top to bottom.

> **tip**
> *If your sewing machine allows you to dictate needle up or needle down position, use needle down.*

8. Place dabs of glue in the seam allowance of the just-sewn patches.

9. Fold over the patches and press to the foundation. Use the mini-iron to create a sharp fold in the fabric at the seamline and to set the glue to the foundation. *Always* iron on the fabric side of the foundation. *Never* iron directly on the printed side (which would smear ink onto your iron and then onto your fabric).

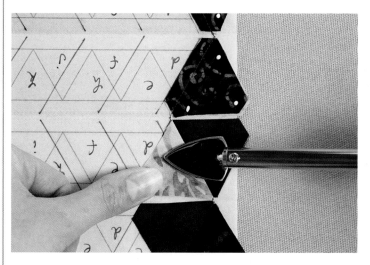

Dab glue in seam allowances; fold open and press.

10. Continue to attach all of the remaining patches using the same step progression:

- Apply glue within the seam allowance of the current patch set.

- Place the next set of patches, right side down.

- Flip the foundation to the printed side and sew the diagonal seamline, top to bottom.

- Flip the foundation back to the fabric side and dab glue in the seam allowance of the just-sewn patches.

- Fold open and iron.

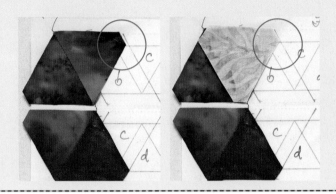

Note: Just as the first patch set extended beyond the seam allowance on the left, the final patch set will extend beyond the seam allowance on the right. Not to worry—it will be trimmed later.

11. After all the patches have been added, trim back any fabric that has extended beyond the seam allowance over the folded creases in the foundation.

JOINING ROWS

1. Fold Row 1 onto Row 2, right sides together. The sharp creases you made will create a perfect alignment of adjoining rows.

Fold first two rows right sides together along crease.

2. Sew the seamline. Begin and end just beyond the outer edge of the seam allowance on the sides. A few backstitches at the beginning and end will help keep row sections from pulling apart when you remove the paper later.

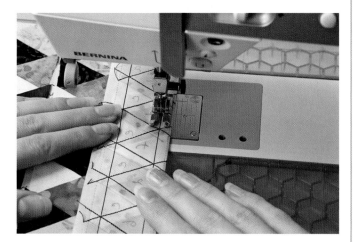

Stitch seam. Backstitch at beginning and end.

> **tip**
> *Sewing just a hair over the seamline into the seam allowance will help create sharper points.*

3. Open the foundation and finger-press.

Unfold foundation and finger-press.

4. Fold Row 2 onto Row 3. Sew, open, and finger-press. Continue to fold and sew until all the rows have been stitched.

Fold and sew remaining rows together.

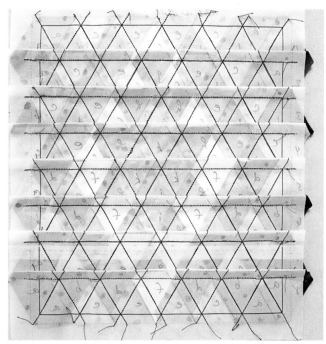

Foundation stitching completed

5. *Trim the excess paper between the rows:* Place the ¼″ mark of your ruler on the seamline. The edge of the ruler should align with the dashed seam allowance printed on the foundation. Be sure that only the section you are trimming extends beyond the ruler edge and that the rest of the foundation and fabric are folded beneath the ruler. Cut off the thin strip of excess paper.

Trim excess paper between rows.

why do this?

This step will make it easier to remove paper from the seam allowances.

6. *Trim the outer border of the foundation/quilt:* Place the ¼″ mark of the ruler on the outer seam line. The edge of the ruler should align with the dashed seam allowance printed on the foundation. Trim.

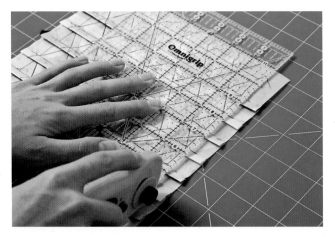

Trim outer borders.

7. Remove the paper. Lightly misting water onto the paper will make for easier removal in places where the glue obstinately holds the fabric to the foundation.

8. Press. You can either press the seams to one side or press them open. Pressing them to one side makes it possible to quilt by stitching in the ditch along both the horizontal and the vertical seams. Pressing the seams open will create flatter seams. This is really a matter of personal preference.

Trimmed foundation, ready for borders

Fold and Sew Projects

All of the projects in this chapter are made using the Fold and Sew technique. For step-by-step directions, see Fold and Sew: A Demonstration with Pyramid Triangles, pages 19–26.

Pyramid Triangle Quilts

TUMBLING BLOCKS ◆ FINISHED FOUNDATION: 7″ × 8″ ◆ TIME: 3 HOURS

Dr. Jeff's Cosmic Blocks, 11½″ × 12½″, Terrie Sandelin, 2007

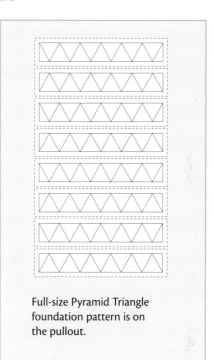

Full-size Pyramid Triangle foundation pattern is on the pullout.

Fabric Requirements

Cream: ⅛ yard or scraps

Medium brown: ⅛ yard or scraps

Dark brown: ⅛ yard or scraps

Light blue: ⅛ yard or scraps

Dark blue: ⅛ yard or scraps

Medium blue for inner border and foundation triangles: ⅛ yard

Blue-black for outer border and foundation triangles: ¼ yard

Backing: 1 fat quarter

Binding: ¼ yard

Cutting Instructions

Letters indicate fabric placement on the quilt layout diagram for the Pyramid Triangle—Tumbling Blocks variation, page 28.

Patches

You may want to add an extra ½″–1″ to each strip length for minor cutting adjustments.

Cut a 1½″ × 2″ rectangle for each patch. Use the Pyramid Triangle patch template on the pullout to trim the rectangles to size.

Cream (A): Cut a strip 1½″ × 32″. Crosscut into 16 patches.

Medium brown (B): Cut a strip 1½" × 32". Crosscut into 16 patches.

Dark brown (C): Cut a strip 1½" × 32". Crosscut into 16 patches.

Light blue (D): Cut a strip 1½" × 16". Crosscut into 8 patches.

Medium blue (E): Cut a strip 1½" × 14". Crosscut into 7 patches.

Dark blue (F): Cut a strip 1½" × 12". Crosscut into 6 patches.

Blue-black background: Cut strips 1½" wide for a total of 70" in length. Crosscut into 35 patches.

Medium blue inner border

Cut 2 strips ¾" × 7½".

Cut 2 strips ¾" × 9".

Blue-black outer border

Cut 2 strips 2¼" × 8".

Cut 2 strips 2¼" × 12½".

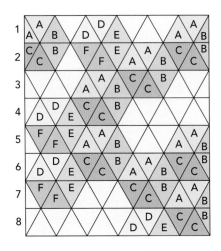

Quilt layout diagram for Pyramid Triangle foundation—Tumbling Blocks variation

Patch requirements: Cut rectangles 1½" × 2". Use template on the pullout to trim to size.

A, B, C–16; D–8; E–7; F–6; Background–35

If desired, enlarge 350% to full size.

Refer to Fold and Sew: A Demonstration with Pyramid Triangles, pages 19–26, for assembly instructions.

FOUR STARS

◆ FINISHED FOUNDATION: **7˝ × 8˝** ◆ TIME: **3 HOURS**

Mardi Gras, 11¾" × 12¾", Terrie Sandelin, quilted by Vickie Bajtelsmit, 2007

Fabric Requirements

Two dark blues: ⅛ yard or scraps of each

Four pinks: ⅛ yard or scraps of each

Three medium blues: ⅛ yard or scraps of each

Two yellows: ⅛ yard or scraps of each

Green: ⅛ yard or scraps

Off-white: ¼ yard

Teal inner border: ⅛ yard

Purple outer border: ¼ yard

Backing: 1 fat quarter

Green binding: ¼ yard

Cutting Instructions

Letters indicate fabric placement on the quilt layout diagram for the Pyramid Triangle—Four Stars variation, page 29.

Outer star points

You may want to add an extra ½"–1" to each strip length for minor cutting adjustments.

Cut a 1½" × 2" rectangle for each patch. Use the Pyramid Triangle patch template on the pullout to trim the rectangles to size.

Two dark blues (A, J): Cut a strip 1½" × 12" of each fabric. Crosscut each into 6 patches.

Two pinks (D, G): Cut a strip 1½" × 12" of each fabric. Crosscut each into 6 patches.

Inner star triangles

You may want to add an extra ½"–1" to each strip length for minor cutting adjustments.

Cut a 1½" × 2" rectangle for each patch. Use the Pyramid Triangle patch template on the pullout to trim the rectangles to size.

Three medium blues (C, F, L): Cut a strip 1½" × 6" of each fabric. Crosscut each into 3 patches.

Two pinks (B, K): Cut a strip 1½" × 6" of each fabric. Crosscut each into 3 patches.

Two yellows (I, E): Cut a strip 1½" × 6" of each fabric. Crosscut each into 3 patches.

Green (H): Cut a strip 1½" × 6". Crosscut into 3 patches.

Background

You may want to add an extra ½"–1" to each strip length for minor cutting adjustments.

Off-white: Cut strips 1½" wide for a total of 112" in length. Crosscut into 56 patches.

Teal inner border

Cut 2 strips ¾" × 7½".

Cut 2 strips ¾" × 9".

Purple outer border

Cut 2 strips 2⅜" × 8".

Cut 2 strips 2⅜" × 12¾".

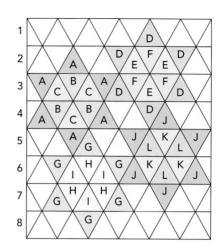

Quilt layout diagram for Pyramid Triangle foundation—Four Stars variation

Patch requirements: Cut rectangles 1½" × 2". Use template on the pullout to trim to size.

A, B, C, D, E, F, G, H, I, J, J–6; K–3; Background–56

If desired, enlarge 350% to full size.

Refer to Fold and Sew: A Demonstration with Pyramid Triangles, pages 19–26, for assembly instructions.

Additional Color Variations

Star Play, 11½″ × 12½″, Terrie Sandelin,
quilted by Audrey Owens, 2007

Star Sparkler, 10¾″ × 11¾″, Liz Marweg, 2007

Star Swirl, 12″ × 12″, Audrey Owens, 2007

Star Dance, 10¾″ × 11¾″, Norma Mill, 2007

HORIZONTAL ROWS

Fabric Requirements

Black: ⅛ yard or scraps

Dark blue: ⅛ yard or scraps

Medium blue: ⅛ yard or scraps

Light blue: ⅛ yard or scraps

Off-white: ⅛ yard or scraps

Burgundy for inner border and foundation triangles: ⅛ yard

Beige for outer border and foundation triangles: ¼ yard

Backing: 1 fat quarter

Binding: ¼ yard

Desert Sand, 11¼″ × 12¼″, Terrie Sandelin, 2007

Cutting Instructions

Letters indicate fabric placement on the quilt layout diagram for the Pyramid Triangle—Horizontal Rows variation, right.

Patches

You may want to add an extra ½″–1″ to each strip length for minor cutting adjustments.

Cut a 1½″ × 2″ rectangle for each patch. Use the Pyramid Triangle patch template on the pullout to trim the rectangles to size.

Black (I): Cut a strip 1½″ × 12″. Crosscut into 6 patches.

Burgundy (B, H, O): Cut a strip 1½″ × 40″. Crosscut into 20 patches.

Off-white (A, G, J, P): Cut strips 1½″ wide for a total of 52″ in length. Crosscut into 26 patches.

Beige (E, L): Cut a strip 1½″ × 24″. Crosscut into 12 patches.

Light blue (D, M): Cut a strip 1½″ × 24″. Crosscut into 12 patches.

Medium blue (F, K): Cut a strip 1½″ × 28″. Crosscut into 14 patches.

Dark blue (C, N): Cut a strip 1½″ × 28″. Crosscut into 14 patches.

Burgundy inner border

Cut 2 strips ¾″ × 7½″.

Cut 2 strips ¾″ × 9″.

Beige outer border

Cut 2 strips 2⅛″ × 8″.

Cut 2 strips 2⅛″ × 12¼″.

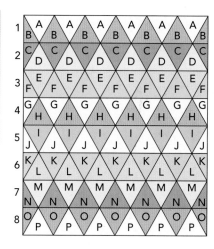

Quilt layout diagram for Pyramid Triangle foundation—Horizontal Rows variation

Patch requirements: Cut rectangles 1½″ × 2″. Use template on the pullout to trim to size.

A, D, E, H, I, L, M, P–6; B, C, F, G, J, K, N, O–7

If desired, enlarge 350% to full size.

Refer to Fold and Sew: A Demonstration with Pyramid Triangles, pages 19–26 for assembly instructions.

MEDALLION

◆ FINISHED FOUNDATION: 7″ × 8″ ◆ TIME: 3 HOURS

Fabric Requirements

Black: ⅛ yard or scraps

Dark blue: ⅛ yard or scraps

Medium blue: ⅛ yard or scraps

Light blue: ⅛ yard or scraps

Off-white: ⅛ yard or scraps

Burgundy for inner border and foundation triangles: ⅛ yard

Beige for outer border and foundation triangles: ¼ yard

Backing: 1 fat quarter

Binding: ¼ yard

Desert Medallion, 11½″ × 12½″, Terrie Sandelin, 2007

Cutting Instructions

Letters indicate fabric placement on the quilt layout diagram for the Pyramid Triangle—Medallion variation, right.

Patches

You may want to add an extra ½″–1″ to each strip length for minor cutting adjustments.

Cut a 1½″ × 2″ rectangle for each patch. Use the Pyramid Triangle patch template on the pullout to trim the rectangles to size.

Black (A): Cut a strip 1½″ × 24″. Crosscut into 12 patches.

Medium blue (B, F, J): Cut a strip 1½″ × 38″. Crosscut into 19 patches.

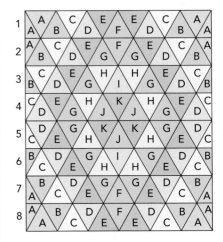

Off-white (C): Cut a strip 1½″ × 32″. Crosscut into 16 patches.

Beige (D, I): Cut a strip 1½″ × 36″. Crosscut into 18 patches.

Burgundy (E, K): Cut a strip 1½″ × 38″. Crosscut into 19 patches.

Dark blue (G): Cut a strip 1½″ × 24″. Crosscut into 12 patches.

Light blue (H): Cut a strip 1½″ × 16″. Crosscut into 8 patches.

Burgundy inner border

Cut 2 strips ¾″ × 7½″.

Cut 2 strips ¾″ × 9″.

Beige outer border

Cut 2 strips 2¼″ × 8″.

Cut 2 strips 2¼″ × 12½″.

Quilt layout diagram for Pyramid Triangle foundation—Medallion variation

Patch requirements: Cut rectangles 1½″ × 2″. Use template on the pullout to trim to size.

A–12, B–12, C–16, D–16, E–16, F–4, G–12, H–8, I–2, J–3, K–3

If desired, enlarge 350% to full size.

Refer to Fold and Sew: A Demonstration with Pyramid Triangles, pages 19–26, for assembly instructions.

DIAGONAL ROWS

◆ **FINISHED FOUNDATION:** 7″ × 8″ ◆ **TIME:** 3 HOURS

Fabric Requirements

Cream: ⅛ yard or scraps

Pale green: ⅛ yard or scraps

Light brown: ⅛ yard or scraps

Four dark browns: ⅛ yard or scraps of each

Dark brown inner border: ⅛ yard

Light to medium green outer border: ¼ yard

Backing: 1 fat quarter

Binding: ¼ yard

Cutting Instructions

Letters indicate fabric placement on the quilt layout diagram for the Pyramid Triangle–Diagonal Rows variation, right.

Patches

You may want to add an extra ½″–1″ to each strip length for minor cutting adjustments.

Cut a 1½″ × 2″ rectangle for each patch. Use the Pyramid Triangle patch template on the pullout to trim the rectangles to size.

Cream (H, M): Cut a strip 1½″ × 32″. Crosscut into 16 patches.

Light brown (A, B, I, L, S, T): Cut a strip 1½″ × 44″. Crosscut into 22 patches.

Dark brown (J, K): Cut a strip 1½″ × 32″. Crosscut into 16 patches.

November Rain, 11¾″ × 12¾″, Terrie Sandelin, 2007

Dark brown (G, N): Cut a strip 1½″ × 28″. Crosscut into 14 patches.

Pale green (C, F, O, R): Cut a strip 1½″ × 36″. Crosscut into 18 patches.

Dark brown (E, P): Cut a strip 1½″ × 20″. Crosscut into 10 patches.

Dark brown (D, Q): Cut a strip 1½″ × 16″. Crosscut into 8 patches.

Dark brown inner border

Cut 2 strips ¾″ × 7½″.

Cut 2 strips ¾″ × 9″.

Light to medium green outer border

Cut 2 strips 2⅜″ × 8″.

Cut 2 strips 2⅜″ × 12¾″.

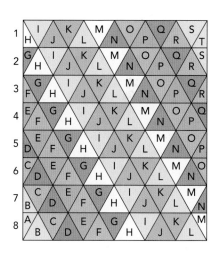

Quilt layout diagram for Pyramid Triangle foundation—Diagonal Rows variation

Patch requirements: Cut rectangles 1½″ × 2″. Use template on the pullout to trim to size.

A–1, B–2, C–3, D–4, E–5, F–6, G–7, H–8, I–8, J–8, K–8, L–8, M–8, N–7, O–6, P–5, Q–4, R–3, S–2, T–1

If desired, enlarge 350% to full size.

Refer to Fold and Sew: A Demonstration with Pyramid Triangles, pages 19–26, for assembly instructions.

TRIANGLE CHARM

Fabric Requirements

Scraps of 104 different fabrics in light, dark, and medium values

White inner border: ⅛ yard

Blue outer border: ¼ yard

Backing: 1 fat quarter

Binding: ¼ yard

Cutting Instructions

There is no quilt layout diagram for this miniature. As you place your patches, alternate light and dark values of fabric. Sprinkle in a scattering of mediums, placing them in either the light or the dark position.

Something Blue, 12¾″ × 13¾″, Terrie Sandelin, 2007

Patches

Cut a 1½″ × 2″ rectangle for each patch. Use the Pyramid Triangle patch template on the pullout to trim the rectangles to size.

Cut 104 patches.

White inner border

Cut 2 strips ¾″ × 7½″.

Cut 2 strips ¾″ × 9″.

Blue outer border

Cut 2 strips 2⅞″ × 8″.

Cut 2 strips 2⅞″ × 13¾″.

Refer to Fold and Sew: A Demonstration with Pyramid Triangles, pages 19–26, for assembly instructions.

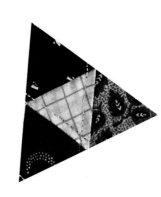

Saturday Mornings, 11¾″ × 11¾″, Terrie Sandelin, quilted by Vickie Bajtelsmit 2007

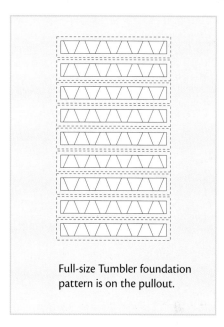

Full-size Tumbler foundation pattern is on the pullout.

The only difference in construction between the Pyramid Triangle quilts and the Tumblers is the shape of the patch template. The Tumbler Triangle patch template on the pullout has a distinct top and bottom (unlike the equilateral Pyramid Triangle patch). Therefore, it must be oriented so that, after sewing, it folds over to properly cover the patch outline on the foundation.

1. Place glue dabs on the fabric side of the foundation as indicated by the green dots in the photograph.

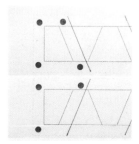

Dab glue on foundation (green dots indicate placement).

2. Set down the first set of patches.

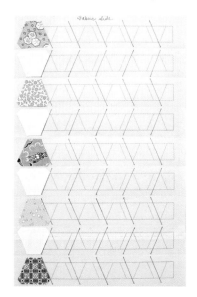

Place first set of patches, right side up.

3. Place the second patch set. Note how the trimmed corner of the patch aligns flat with the dashed seam allowance lines on the foundation.

Note alignment of second patch set.

tip

When the patch aligns so that the wide edge folds over to the top, the corner edge will align with the top seam allowance. When the patch aligns so that the wide edge folds over to the bottom, the corner edge will align with the bottom.

DIAGONAL ROWS

Fabric Requirements

Two dark browns: ⅛ yard or scraps of each

Two medium browns: ⅛ yard or scraps of each

Two light browns: ⅛ yard or scraps of each

Dark pink: ⅛ yard or scraps

Two medium pinks: ⅛ yard or scraps of each

Light pink: ⅛ yard or scraps

Dark brown inner border: ⅛ yard

Pink outer border: ¼ yard

Backing: 1 fat quarter

Binding: ¼ yard

Yesterday's Roses, 11¾″ × 11¾″, Terrie Sandelin, 2007

Cutting Instructions

Letters indicate fabric placement on the quilt layout diagram for the Tumbler–Diagonal Rows variation, page 37.

Patches

You may want to add an extra ½″–1″ to each strip length for minor cutting adjustments.

Cut a 1¼″ × 1¾″ rectangle for each patch. Use the Tumbler Triangle patch template on the pullout to trim the rectangles to size.

Dark brown (A, S): Cut a strip 1¼″ × 3½″. Crosscut into 2 patches.

Dark brown (C, Q): Cut a strip 1¼″ × 10½″. Crosscut into 6 patches.

Medium brown (E, O): Cut a strip 1¼″ × 17½″. Crosscut into 10 patches.

Medium brown (G, M): Cut a strip 1¼″ × 24½″. Crosscut into 14 patches.

Light brown (B, R): Cut a strip 1¼″ × 7″. Crosscut into 4 patches.

Light brown (H, L): Cut a strip 1¼″ × 28″. Crosscut into 16 patches.

Dark pink (J): Cut a strip 1¼″ × 15¾″. Crosscut into 9 patches.

Medium pink (D, P): Cut a strip 1¼″ × 14″. Crosscut into 8 patches.

Medium pink (I, K): Cut a strip 1¼″ × 31½″. Crosscut into 18 patches.

Light pink (F, N): Cut a strip 1¼″ × 21″. Crosscut into 12 patches.

Dark brown inner border

The border measurements listed here are for straight borders. If you choose to miter your borders, add length accordingly.

Cut 2 strips ¾″ × 7½″.

Cut 2 strips ¾″ × 8″.

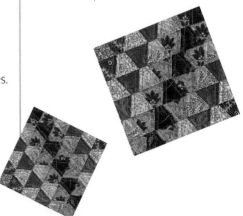

Pink outer border

The border measurements listed here are for straight borders. If you choose to miter your borders, add length accordingly.

Cut 2 strips 2⅜″ × 8″.

Cut 2 strips 2⅜″ × 11¾″.

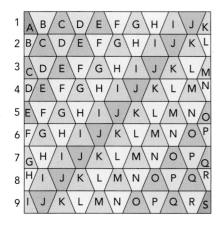

Quilt layout diagram for Tumbler foundation—Diagonal Rows variation

Patch requirements: Cut patches 1¼″ × 1¾″.

A–1, B–2, C–3, D–4, E–5, F–6, G–7, H–8, I–9, J–9, K–9, L–8, M–7, N–6, O–5, P–4, Q–3, R–2, S–1

If desired, enlarge 350% to full size.

Refer to Fold and Sew: A Demonstration with Pyramid Triangles, pages 19–26, for assembly instructions. See Tumbler Quilts, page 35, for a guide to glue and fabric placement on the patches.

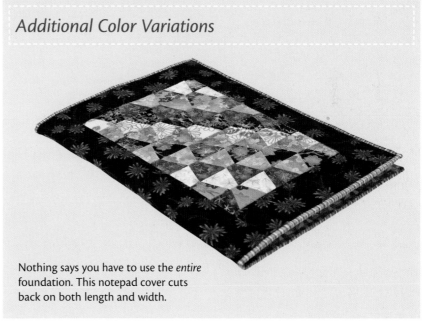

Additional Color Variations

Nothing says you have to use the *entire* foundation. This notepad cover cuts back on both length and width.

MEDALLION

◆ **FINISHED FOUNDATION:** 7″ × 7″ ◆ **TIME:** 3 HOURS

Fabric Requirements

Gold: scraps

Dark blue with gold print: ⅛ yard or scraps

Red print for outer border and foundation: ¼ yard

Medium blue for inner border and foundation: ⅛ yard

Dark blue: ⅛ yard or scraps

Red/orange: scraps

Light blue background: ⅛ yard

Backing: 1 fat quarter

Binding: ⅛ yard

Eagle Dawn, 11½″ × 11½″, Terrie Sandelin, 2007

Cutting Instructions

> Letters indicate fabric placement on the quilt layout diagram for the Tumbler—Medallion variation, right.

Patches

You may want to add an extra ½″–1″ to each strip length for minor cutting adjustments.

Cut a 1¼″ × 1¾″ rectangle for each patch. Use the Tumbler Triangle patch template on the pullout to trim the rectangles to size.

Gold (A): Cut a strip 1¼″ × 7″. Crosscut into 4 patches.

Dark blue with gold print (B): Cut a strip 1¼″ × 21″. Crosscut into 12 patches.

Red print (C): Cut a strip 1¼″ × 31½″. Crosscut into 18 patches.

Medium blue (D): Cut a strip 1¼″ × 21″. Crosscut into 12 patches.

Dark blue (E): Cut a strip 1¼″ × 7″. Crosscut into 4 patches.

Red/orange (F): Cut a strip 1¼″ × 1¾″. Cut 1 patch.

Light blue (background): Cut strips 1¼″ wide for a total of 84″ in length. Crosscut into 48 patches.

Medium blue inner border

Cut 2 strips ¾″ × 7½″.

Cut 2 strips ¾″ × 8″.

Red print outer border

Cut 2 strips 2¼″ × 8″.

Cut 2 strips 2¼″ × 11½″.

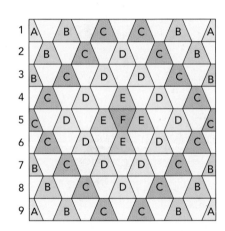

Quilt layout diagram for Tumbler foundation—Medallion variation

Patch requirements: Cut patches 1¼″ × 1¾″.

A–4, B–12, C–18, D–12, E–4, F–1, Background–48

If desired, enlarge 350% to full size.

Refer to Fold and Sew: A Demonstration with Pyramid Triangles, pages 19–26, for assembly instructions. See Tumbler Quilts, page 35, for a guide to glue and fabric placement on the patches.

TUMBLER CHARM

◆ **FINISHED FOUNDATION:** **7″ × 7″** ◆ **TIME:** **3 HOURS**

Fabric Requirements

Scraps of 99 different fabrics

Green inner border: ⅛ yard

Burgundy outer border: ¼ yard

Backing: 1 fat quarter

Binding: ⅛ yard

Cutting Instructions

There is no quilt layout diagram for this miniature. Place your fabrics randomly for a fun, scrappy quilt.

Charmed to Greet You, 13″ × 13″, Terrie Sandelin, 2007

Patches

Cut a 1¼″ × 1¾″ rectangle for each patch. Use the Tumbler Triangle patch template on the pullout to trim the rectangles to size.

Cut 99 patches.

Green inner border

Cut 2 strips ¾″ × 7½″.

Cut 2 strips ¾″ × 8″.

Burgundy outer border

Cut 2 strips 3″ × 8″.

Cut 2 strips 3″ × 13″.

Refer to Fold and Sew: A Demonstration with Pyramid Triangles pages 19–26, for assembly instructions. See Tumbler Quilts, page 35, for a guide to glue and fabric placement on the patches.

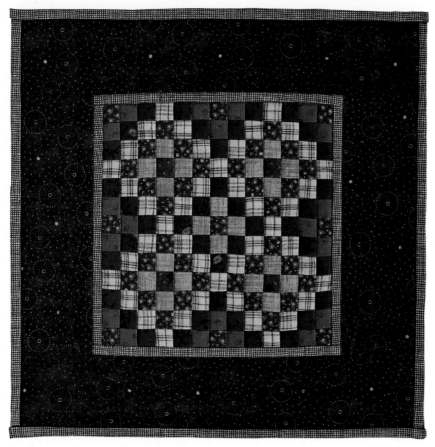

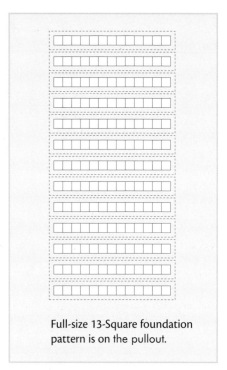

Full-size 13-Square foundation pattern is on the pullout.

Hoedown, 11½″ × 11½″, Terrie Sandelin, 2007

The 13-Square pattern is one of the easiest and fastest of all the miniatures. The patches are cut 1-inch square— no template needed. The method of construction is the same as with the Pyramid Triangle and Tumbler, but the stitch line goes straight from top to bottom, with no stops or turns. This is the perfect mini for a fast and easy project.

tip

Be sure to place the patch placement lettering to the right of the drawn seam allowance.

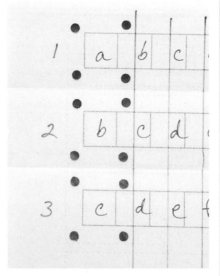

Dab glue on foundation (green dots indicate placement).

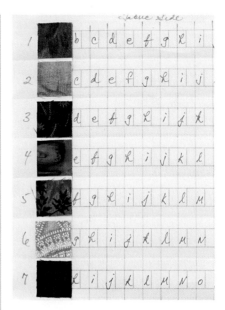

First set of patches in place

TRIP AROUND THE WORLD

◆ **FINISHED FOUNDATION:** 6½″ × 6½″ ◆ **TIME:** 2½ HOURS

Fabric Requirements

Two light taupes: ⅛ yard or scraps of each

Six medium taupes: ⅛ yard or scraps of each

Five dark taupes: ⅛ yard or scraps of each

Dark brown inner border: ⅛ yard

Light brown outer border: ¼ yard

Backing: 1 fat quarter

Binding: ¼ yard

Kyoto Dreams, 11¼″ × 11¼″, Terrie Sandelin, quilted by Vickie Bajtelsmit, 2007

Cutting Instructions

Letters indicate fabric placement on the quilt layout diagram for the 13-Square–Trip Around the World variation, right.

Patches

You may want to add an extra ½″–1″ to each strip length for minor cutting adjustments.

Cut each patch 1″ × 1″.

Dark taupe (D): Cut a strip 1″ × 16″. Crosscut into 16 patches.

Dark taupe (F): Cut a strip 1″ × 24″. Crosscut into 24 patches.

Dark taupe (H): Cut a strip 1″ × 20″. Crosscut into 20 patches.

Dark taupe (I): Cut a strip 1″ × 16″. Crosscut into 16 patches.

Dark taupe (K): Cut a strip 1″ × 8″. Crosscut into 8 patches.

Medium taupe (A): Cut a strip 1″ × 4″. Crosscut into 4 patches.

Medium taupe (C): Cut a strip 1″ × 12″. Crosscut into 12 patches.

Medium taupe (E): Cut a strip 1″ × 20″. Crosscut into 20 patches.

Medium taupe (G): Cut a strip 1″ × 24″. Crosscut into 24 patches.

Medium taupe (L): Cut a strip 1″ × 4″. Crosscut into 4 patches.

Medium taupe (M): Cut a strip 1″ × 1″. Cut 1 patch.

Light taupe (B): Cut a strip 1″ × 8″. Crosscut into 8 patches.

Light taupe (J): Cut a strip 1″ × 12″. Crosscut into 12 patches.

Dark brown inner border

Cut 2 strips ¾″ × 7″.

Cut 2 strips ¾″ × 7½″.

Light brown outer border

Cut 2 strips 2⅜″ × 7½″.

Cut 2 strips 2⅜″ × 11¼″.

1	A	B	C	D	E	F	G	F	E	D	C	B	A
2	B	C	D	E	F	G	H	G	F	E	D	C	B
3	C	D	E	F	G	H	I	H	G	F	E	D	C
4	D	E	F	G	H	I	J	I	H	G	F	E	D
5	E	F	G	H	I	J	K	J	I	H	G	F	E
6	F	G	H	I	J	K	L	K	J	I	H	G	F
7	G	H	I	J	K	L	M	L	K	J	I	H	G
8	F	G	H	I	J	K	L	K	J	I	H	G	F
9	E	F	G	H	I	J	K	J	I	H	G	F	E
10	D	E	F	G	H	I	J	I	H	G	F	E	D
11	C	D	E	F	G	H	I	H	G	F	E	D	C
12	B	C	D	E	F	G	H	G	F	E	D	C	B
13	A	B	C	D	E	F	G	F	E	D	C	B	A

Quilt layout diagram for 13-Square foundation—Trip Around the World variation

Patch requirements: Cut squares 1″ × 1″.

A–4, B–8, C–12, D–16, E–20, F–24, G–24, H–20, I–16, J–12, K–8, L–4, M–1

If desired, enlarge 325% to full size.

Refer to Fold and Sew: A Demonstration with Pyramid Triangles, pages 19–26, for assembly instructions. See 13-Square Quilts, page 40, for a guide to glue placement on the patches.

DIAMOND-ON-A-SQUARE

◆ FINISHED FOUNDATION: 6½″ × 6½″ ◆ TIME: 2½ HOURS

Fabric Requirements

Three dark browns: ⅛ yard or scraps of each

Two tans: ⅛ yard or scraps of each

Burgundy: ⅛ yard or scraps

Two medium browns: ⅛ yard or scraps of each

Light brown: ⅛ yard or scraps

Cream: ⅛ yard or scraps

Cream/beige: ⅛ yard or scraps

Dark brown inner border: ⅛ yard

Medium brown outer border: ¼ yard

Backing: 1 fat quarter

Binding: ¼ yard

Cutting Instructions

> Letters indicate fabric placement on the quilt layout diagram for the 13-Square—Diamond-on-a-Square variation, right.

Patches

You may want to add an extra ½″–1″ to each strip length for minor cutting adjustments.

Cut each patch 1″ × 1″.

Dark brown (A): Cut a strip 1″ × 8″. Crosscut into 8 patches.

Tan (B, K): Cut a strip 1″ × 28″. Crosscut into 28 patches.

Tan (C, Q): Cut a strip 1″ × 17″. Crosscut into 17 patches.

Burgundy (D, L, P): Cut a strip 1″ × 28″. Crosscut into 28 patches.

Dark brown (E): Cut a strip 1″ × 8″. Crosscut into 8 patches.

Dark brown (F): Cut a strip 1″ × 8″. Crosscut into 8 patches.

Medium brown (G): Cut a strip 1″ × 8″. Crosscut into 8 patches.

Light brown (H): Cut a strip 1″ × 8″. Crosscut into 8 patches.

Cream (I): Cut a strip 1″ × 12″. Crosscut into 12 patches.

Cream/beige (J, N): Cut a strip 1″ × 20″. Crosscut into 20 patches.

Medium brown (M, O): Cut a strip 1″ × 24″. Crosscut into 24 patches.

Dark brown inner border

Cut 2 strips ¾″ × 7″.

Cut 2 strips ¾″ × 7½″.

Medium brown outer border

Cut 2 strips 2⅝″ × 7½″.

Cut 2 strips 2⅝″ × 11¾″.

Mountain Mist, 11¾″ × 11¾″, Terrie Sandelin, 2007

1	A	B	C	B	C	B	A	B	C	B	C	B	A
2	B	D	E	F	G	H	L	H	G	F	E	D	B
3	C	E	K	J	I	L	M	L	I	J	K	E	C
4	B	F	J	I	L	M	N	M	L	I	J	F	B
5	C	G	I	L	M	N	O	N	M	L	I	G	C
6	B	H	L	M	N	O	P	O	N	M	L	H	B
7	A	L	M	N	O	P	Q	P	O	N	M	L	A
8	B	H	L	M	N	O	P	O	N	M	L	H	B
9	C	G	I	L	M	N	O	N	M	L	I	G	C
10	B	F	J	I	L	M	N	M	L	I	J	F	B
11	C	E	K	J	I	L	M	L	I	J	K	E	C
12	B	D	E	F	G	H	L	H	G	F	E	D	B
13	A	B	C	B	C	B	A	B	C	B	C	B	A

Quilt layout diagram for 13-Square foundation—Diamond-on-a-Square variation

Patch requirements: Cut squares 1″ × 1″.

A–8, B–24, C–16, D–4, E–8, F–8, G–8, H–8, I–12, J–8, K–4, L–20, M–16, N–12, O–8, P–4, Q–1

If desired, enlarge 325% to full size.

Refer to Fold and Sew: A Demonstration with Pyramid Triangles, pages 19–26, for assembly instructions. See 13-Square Quilts, page 40, for a guide to glue placement on the patches.

FOUR CROSSES ON-POINT

◆ **FINISHED FOUNDATION:** 6¹/₂″ × 6¹/₂″ ◆ **TIME:** 2¹/₂ HOURS

Fabric Requirements

Dark brown: ⅛ yard or scraps

Medium dark brown: ⅛ yard or scraps

Two medium browns: ⅛ yard or scraps of each

Light brown: ⅛ yard or scraps

Two creams: ⅛ yard or scraps of each

Dark brown inner border: ⅛ yard

Medium brown outer border: ¼ yard

Backing: 1 fat quarter

Binding: ¼ yard

Cutting Instructions

Letters indicate fabric placement on the quilt layout diagram for the 13-Square—Four Crosses On-Point variation, right.

Patches

You may want to add an extra ½″–1″ to each strip length for minor cutting adjustments.

Cut each patch 1″ × 1″.

Dark brown (A, H): Cut a strip 1″ × 36″. Crosscut into 36 patches.

Medium dark brown (B): Cut a strip 1″ × 8″. Crosscut into 8 patches.

Medium brown (C, G, J): Cut a strip 1″ × 48″. Crosscut into 48 patches.

Medium brown (D): Cut a strip 1″ × 16″. Crosscut into 16 patches.

Light brown (E): Cut a strip 1″ × 20″. Crosscut into 20 patches.

Cream (F): Cut a strip 1″ × 24″. Crosscut into 24 patches.

Cream (I, K): Cut a strip 1″ × 17″. Crosscut into 17 patches.

Dark brown inner border

Cut 2 strips ¾″ × 7″.

Cut 2 strips ¾″ × 7½″.

Medium brown outer border

Cut 2 strips 2½″ × 7½″.

Cut 2 strips 2½″ × 11½″.

Chestnut Fall, 11½″ × 11½″, Terrie Sandelin, 2007

Patch requirements: Cut squares 1″ × 1″.

A–4, B–8, C–12, D–16, E–20, F–24, G–32, H–32, I–16, J–4, K–1

If desired, enlarge 340% to full size.

Refer to Fold and Sew: A Demonstration with Pyramid Triangles, pages 19–26, for assembly instructions. See 13-Square Quilts, page 40, for a guide to glue placement on the patches.

Additional Color Variations

Tote bags are a great way to display your minis. These 13-Square patterns finish at 6½″ inches—the perfect size for an outer pocket.

1	A	B	C	D	E	F	G	F	E	D	C	B	A
2	B	C	D	E	F	G	H	G	F	E	D	C	B
3	C	D	E	F	G	H	I	H	G	F	E	D	C
4	D	E	F	G	H	I	J	I	H	G	F	E	D
5	E	F	G	H	G	H	I	H	G	H	G	F	E
6	F	G	H	I	H	G	H	G	H	I	H	G	F
7	G	H	I	J	I	H	K	H	I	J	I	H	G
8	F	G	H	I	H	G	H	G	H	I	H	G	F
9	E	F	G	H	G	H	I	H	G	H	G	F	E
10	D	E	F	G	H	I	J	I	H	G	F	E	D
11	C	D	E	F	G	H	I	H	G	F	E	D	C
12	B	C	D	E	F	G	H	G	F	E	D	C	B
13	A	B	C	D	E	F	G	F	E	D	C	B	A

Quilt layout diagram for 13-Square foundation—Four Crosses On-Point variation

FIVE CROSSES

◆ **FINISHED FOUNDATION:** 6½˝ × 6½˝ ◆ **TIME:** 2½ HOURS

Fabric Requirements

Salmon: ⅛ yard or scraps

Dark gray: ⅛ yard or scraps

Burgundy for inner border and foundation squares: ⅛ yard

Off-white: ⅛ yard or scraps

Brown: ⅛ yard or scraps

Beige outer border: ¼ yard

Backing: 1 fat quarter

Binding: ¼ yard

Cutting Instructions

Letters indicate fabric placement on the quilt layout diagram for the 13-Square—Five Crosses variation, right.

Patches

You may want to add an extra ½˝–1˝ to each strip length for minor cutting adjustments.

Cut each patch 1˝ × 1˝.

Salmon (A, F, I): Cut a strip 1˝ × 25˝. Crosscut into 25 patches.

Dark gray (B): Cut a strip 1˝ × 20˝. Crosscut into 20 patches.

Burgundy (C, G, J): Cut a strip 1˝ × 44˝. Crosscut into 44 patches.

Off-white (D): Cut a strip 1˝ × 44˝. Crosscut into 44 patches.

Brown (E, H): Cut a strip 1˝ × 36˝. Crosscut into 36 patches.

Promises, 11¾˝ × 11¾˝, Terrie Sandelin, 2007

Burgundy inner borders

Cut 2 strips ¾˝ × 7˝.

Cut 2 strips ¾˝ × 7½˝.

Beige outer border

Cut 2 strips 2⅝˝ × 7½˝.

Cut 2 strips 2⅝˝ × 11¾˝.

1	A	B	C	D	C	B	A	B	C	D	C	B	A
2	B	C	D	E	D	C	B	C	D	E	D	C	B
3	C	D	E	F	E	D	C	D	E	F	E	D	C
4	D	E	F	J	F	E	D	E	F	J	F	E	D
5	C	D	E	F	E	D	G	D	E	F	E	D	C
6	B	C	D	E	D	G	H	G	D	E	D	C	B
7	A	B	C	D	G	H	I	H	G	D	C	B	A
8	B	C	D	E	D	G	H	G	D	E	D	C	B
9	C	D	E	F	E	D	G	D	E	F	E	D	C
10	D	E	F	J	F	E	D	E	F	J	F	E	D
11	C	D	E	F	E	D	C	D	E	F	E	D	C
12	B	C	D	E	D	C	B	C	D	E	D	C	B
13	A	B	C	D	C	B	A	B	C	D	C	B	A

Quilt layout diagram for 13-Square foundation—Five Crosses variation

Patch requirements: Cut squares 1˝ × 1˝.

A–8, B–20, C–32, D–44, E–32, F–16, G–8, H–4, I–1, J–4

If desired, enlarge 325% to full size.

Refer to Fold and Sew: A Demonstration with Pyramid Triangles, pages 19–26, for assembly instructions. See 13-Square Quilts, page 40, for a guide to glue placement on the patches.

DIAGONAL ROWS

◆ **FINISHED FOUNDATION:** $6\frac{1}{2}'' \times 6\frac{1}{2}''$ ◆ **TIME:** $2\frac{1}{2}$ **HOURS**

Fabric Requirements

Dark blue: ⅛ yard or scraps

Medium blue: ⅛ yard or scraps

Two dark purples: ⅛ yard or scraps of each

Medium blue/purple: ⅛ yard or scraps

Light purple: ⅛ yard or scraps

Two dark greens: ⅛ yard or scraps of each

Blue: ⅛ yard or scraps

Purple: ⅛ yard or scraps

Green inner border: ⅛ yard

Purple outer border: ¼ yard

Backing: 1 fat quarter

Binding: ¼ yard

Cutting Instructions

Letters indicate fabric placement on the quilt layout diagram for the 13-Square—Diagonal Rows variation, right.

Patches

You may want to add an extra ½"–1" to each strip length for minor cutting adjustments.

Cut each patch 1" × 1".

Dark blue (A, Y): Cut a strip 1" × 2". Crosscut into 2 patches.

Medium blue (B, X): Cut a strip 1" × 4". Crosscut into 4 patches.

Dark purple (C, W): Cut a strip 1" × 6". Crosscut into 6 patches.

Medium blue/purple (D, V): Cut a strip 1" × 8". Crosscut into 8 patches.

Dark green (E, U): Cut a strip 1" × 10". Crosscut into 10 patches.

Dark green (I, Q): Cut a strip 1" × 18". Crosscut into 18 patches.

Light purple (F, H, L, N, R, T): Cut strips 1" wide for a total of 52" in length. Crosscut into 52 patches.

Dark purple (G, M, S): Cut a strip 1" × 27". Crosscut into 27 patches.

Blue (J, P): Cut a strip 1" × 20". Crosscut into 20 patches.

Purple (K, O): Cut a strip 1" × 22". Crosscut into 22 patches.

Green inner border

Cut 2 strips ¾" × 7.

Cut 2 strips ¾" × 7½".

Purple outer border

Cut 2 strips 2½" × 7½".

Cut 2 strips 2½" × 11½".

Shadowfall, 11½" × 11½", Terrie Sandelin, 2007

1	A	B	C	D	E	F	G	H	I	J	K	L	M
2	B	C	D	E	F	G	H	I	J	K	L	M	N
3	C	D	E	F	G	H	I	J	K	L	M	N	O
4	D	E	F	G	H	I	J	K	L	M	N	O	P
5	E	F	G	H	I	J	K	L	M	N	O	P	Q
6	F	G	H	I	J	K	L	M	N	O	P	Q	R
7	G	H	I	J	K	L	M	N	O	P	Q	R	S
8	H	I	J	K	L	M	N	O	P	Q	R	S	T
9	I	J	K	L	M	N	O	P	Q	R	S	T	U
10	J	K	L	M	N	O	P	Q	R	S	T	U	V
11	K	L	M	N	O	P	Q	R	S	T	U	V	W
12	L	M	N	O	P	Q	R	S	T	U	V	W	X
13	M	N	O	P	Q	R	S	T	U	V	W	X	Y

Quilt layout diagram for 13-Square-foundation—Diagonal Rows variation

Patch requirements: Cut squares 1" × 1".

A–1, B–2, C–3, D–4, E–5, F–6, G–7, H–8, I–9, J–10, K–11, L–12, M–13, N–12, O–11, P–10, Q–9, R–8, S–7, T–6, U–5, V–4, W–3, X–2, Y–1

If desired, enlarge 325% to full size.

Refer to Fold and Sew: A Demonstration with Pyramid Triangles, pages 19–26, for assembly instructions. See 13-Square Quilts, page 40, for a guide to glue placement on the patches.

◆ FINISHED FOUNDATION: $7^{3}/_{4}″ \times 7^{3}/_{4}″$ ◆ TIME: $5^{1}/_{2}$ HOURS

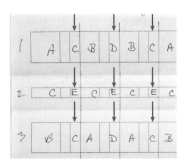

Full-size Sashed Squares foundation pattern is on the pullout.

Been There, Done That, 14″ × 14″, Terrie Sandelin, quilted by Vickie Bajtelsmit, 2007. Believe it or not, this geometrically bold design that looks so modern actually re-creates the layout and coloring of an 1820s quilt backing!

MARKING THE FOUNDATION

Although the basic construction of the Sashed Squares foundation is the same as the 13-Square foundation, the tiny pieces of this quilt (those yellow sashing squares finish at ¼″) present a unique challenge for marking the foundation.

Because the sashing strips are ¼″ wide, you can use the printed line of the foundation as the seam allowance guide for the patches that precede them. Draw the seam allowance lines only for the seamlines that follow the sashing patches. Then place a patch on the first square. Notice how the seam allowance fabric of the previous patch completely covers the sashing strip? Those ¼″ sashing widths mean that if you mark a letter in either the sashing strip or the sashing square, the seam allowance fabric of the previous patch will cover the letter. To avoid this, write the letter in the next patch over. Placing it to the left of the drawn seam allowance line is a good reminder that it applies to the previous patch.

Letter placement for narrow sashing strips and squares

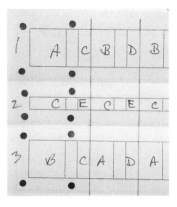

Dab glue on foundation
(green dots indicate placement).

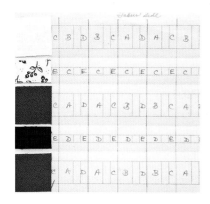

First patch set in place and aligned with printed seamline of next patch over

> ## tip
> With this mini, press the seams open to reduce seam bulk.

Fabric Requirements

Red: ⅛ yard or scraps

White: ⅛ yard or scraps

Red-on-white print: ⅛ yard or scraps

Yellow inner border and foundation: ⅛ yard

Black outer border and foundation: ¼ yard

Backing: 1 fat quarter

Binding: ¼ yard

Cutting Instructions

Letters indicate fabric placement on the quilt layout diagram for Sashed Squares, right.

Large squares

You may want to add an extra ½″–1″ to each strip length for minor cutting adjustments.

Cut each large square patch 1¼″ × 1¼″.

> White (A): Cut a strip 1¼″ × 40″. Crosscut into 32 patches.
>
> Red (B): Cut a strip 1¼″ × 40″. Crosscut into 32 patches.

Small squares

You may want to add an extra ½″–1″ to each strip length for minor cutting adjustments.

Cut each small square patch ¾″ × ¾″.

> Yellow (E): Cut a strip ¾″ × 36¾″. Crosscut into 49 patches.

Rectangles

You may want to add an extra ½″–1″ to each strip length for minor cutting adjustments.

Cut each rectangle ¾″ × 1¼″.

> Black (D): Cut strips ¾″ wide for a total of 60″ in length. Crosscut into 48 patches.
>
> Red-on-white print (C): Cut strips ¾″ wide for a total of 80″ in length. Crosscut into 64 patches.

Yellow for inner border

Cut 2 strips ¾″ × 8¼″.

Cut 2 strips ¾″ × 8¾″.

Black for outer border

Cut 2 strips 3⅛″ × 8¾″.

Cut 2 strips 3⅛″ × 14″.

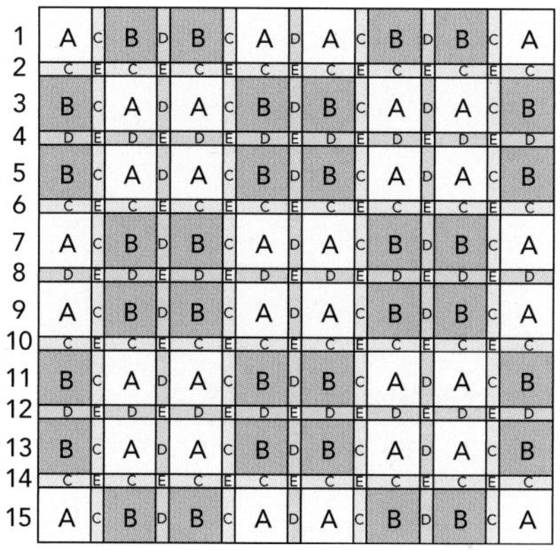

1	A	c	B	d	B	A	d	A	c	B	d	B	c	d	A
2	c	E	c	E	c	E	c	E	c	E	c	E	c	E	c
3	B		A	c	A	d	B		B	c	A	d	A	c	B
4	D	E	D	E	D	E	D	E	D	E	D	E	D	E	D
5	B		A	c	A	d	B		B	c	A	d	A		
6	c	E	c	E	c	E	c	E	c	E	c	E	c	E	c
7	A	c	B	d	B	A	d	A	c	B	d	B	c	d	A
8	D	E	D	E	D	E	D	E	D	E	D	E	D	E	D
9	A	c	B	d	B	A	d	A	c	B	d	B	c	d	A
10	c	E	c	E	c	E	c	E	c	E	c	E	c	E	c
11	B		A	c	A	d	B		B	c	A	d	A	c	B
12	D	E	D	E	D	E	D	E	D	E	D	E	D	E	D
13	B		A	c	A	d	B		B	c	A	d	A		
14	c	E	c	E	c	E	c	E	c	E	c	E	c	E	c
15	A	c	B	d	B	A	d	A	c	B	d	B	c	d	A

Quilt layout diagram for Sashed Squares

Patch requirements:
Cut squares 1¼″ × 1¼″. A–32, B–32
Cut rectangles ¾″ × 1½″. C–64, D–48
Cut squares ¾″ × ¾″. E–49

If desired, enlarge 385% to full size.

Refer to Fold and Sew: A Demonstration with Pyramid Triangles, pages 19–26, for assembly instructions. See Sashed Squares, page 46, for a guide to glue placement on the patches.

Sew and Skip Projects

Instead of sewing from one side of the foundation to the other in a continuous line, with Sew and Skip you will occasionally stop, lift the needle, move the foundation beneath the presser foot, and then drop the needle back down where you once again need to stitch.

The foundation sew line diagrams illustrate where you need to sew (red lines) and where you need to skip (green lines). Notice that you continue to sew both on the printed seamline and through the adjacent seam allowances.

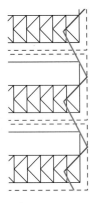

Flying Geese foundation sew line diagram

Red lines indicate sew lines. Green lines indicate skips.

The technique is simple. Follow the directions in Fold and Sew: A Demonstration with Pyramid Triangles, pages 19–26, but with the following exceptions:

1. Begin sewing where indicated on the foundation sew line diagram.

2. After sewing through the seam allowance, lift the needle and the presser foot, move the foundation, and then drop the needle back in the seam allowance of the next sew line.

3. Lower the presser foot and continue sewing.

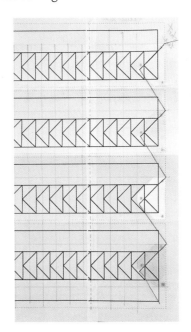

Sew and Skip stitching on printed side of foundation (red thread used for demonstration purposes)

Sew and Skip stitching on fabric side of foundation

> **tip**
>
> *If your sewing machine allows you to dictate needle up or needle down, choose needle up.*

EVERLASTING TREE

◆ **FINISHED FOUNDATION:** 6¾" × 8¼" ◆ **TIME:** 2 HOURS

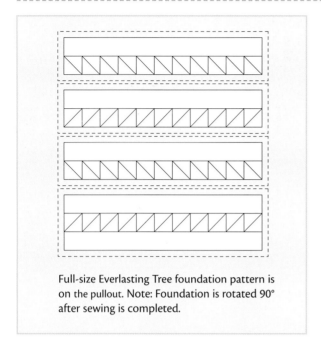

Full-size Everlasting Tree foundation pattern is on the pullout. Note: Foundation is rotated 90° after sewing is completed.

Portal, 11½" × 13", Terrie Sandelin, 2007

Fabric Requirements

Dark purple: ⅛ yard or scraps

Cream: ⅛ yard or scraps

Teal print: ⅛ yard or scraps

Pale purple print: ⅛ yard or scraps

Dark purple print: ⅛ yard or scraps

Mottled: ⅛ yard or scraps

Turquoise inner border: ⅛ yard

Dark green outer border: ¼ yard

Backing: 1 fat quarter

Binding: ⅛ yard

Cutting Instructions

There is no quilt layout diagram for this miniature. As you place your triangle patches, alternate light and dark.

Triangles

You may want to add an extra ½" to each half-square triangle strip length for minor cutting adjustments.

Trim the half-square triangle dog ears using either The Ruler Method: Trimming Half-Square Triangles, page 50, or the ¾" Finished Half-Square Triangle patch template on the pullout.

Cream: Cut a strip 1⅝" × 35¾". Crosscut into 22 squares; cut once on the diagonal to create 44 half-square triangles.

Teal print: Cut a strip 1⅝" × 17⅞". Crosscut into 11 squares; cut once on the diagonal to create 22 half-square triangles.

Dark purple: Cut a strip 1⅝" × 17⅞". Crosscut into 11 squares; cut once on the diagonal to create 22 half-square triangles.

Sashing strips

Pale purple print: Cut a strip 1¼" × 8¾".

Dark purple print: Cut 2 strips 1¼" × 8¾".

Mottled print: Cut 2 strips 1¼" × 8¾".

Turquoise inner border

Cut 2 strips ¾" × 7¼".

Cut 2 strips ¾" × 9¼".

Dark green outer border

Cut 2 strips 2⅜" × 7¾".

Cut 2 strips 2⅜" × 13".

the ruler method:
trimming half-square triangles

Many of the quilts (such as Everlasting Tree, Flying Geese, and Square-in-a-Square) use half-square triangles with trimmed dog ears. Here is an easy method for cutting and trimming multiple patches at once.

1. Layer your fabrics 4 deep. Cut a square patch the size indicated in the project instructions for your quilt.

2. Cut the square in half along the diagonal.

3. Line up a ruler so that the square sides of the triangle match the measurement indicated in the chart. Trim off the dog ears.

TRIMMING HALF-SQUARE TRIANGLES

SHORT EDGE OF FINISHED TRIANGLE	CUT SQUARE	TRIM MEASUREMENT
½″	1⅜″	1″
¾″	1⅝″	1¼″
1¼″	2⅛″	1¾″

Dimensions for cutting and trimming half-square triangles

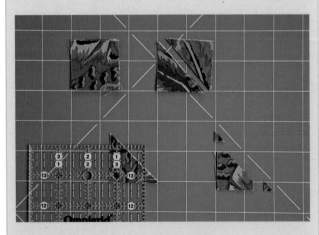

Cutting and trimming half-square triangles

PREPARING THE FOUNDATION

1. As with the basic Fold and Sew patterns, pages 19–21, line up adjoining seamlines that are separated by a seam allowance. Then fold and crease.

2. Use a red extra-fine permanent marker to draw ¼″ seam allowance lines down the long edge of the triangle rows on the sides that do not have printed seam allowances already marked.

3. Draw perpendicular lines to mark the ¼″ seam allowances on the half-square triangle squares.

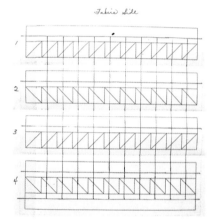

Draw seam allowances in red.

4. Once the initial light/dark pattern of fabric placement is established, it will be clear which fabrics go where. Therefore, there is no need for a quilt layout diagram. It does help, however, to mark X's on the foundation to indicate the dark fabric placement of the first patch set.

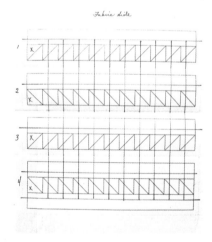

Mark dark fabric placement with X's.

SEWING THE FOUNDATION

Sew Triangle Strips

1. Place glue dabs on the foundation as indicated by the green dots in the photograph.

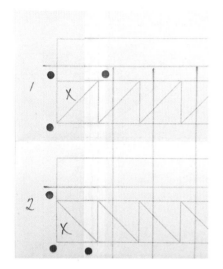

Dab glue on foundation (green dots indicate placement).

2. Place the first set of fabrics *right side up* on the foundation.

3. Dab glue onto the diagonal seam allowances of the just-placed patches.

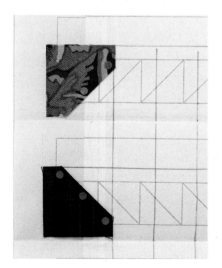

Dab glue on patches (green dots indicate placement).

4. Place the second set of patches on top of the first.

5. Flip the foundation to the printed side and sew as indicated by the foundation sew line diagram.

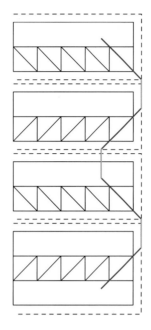

Red lines indicate sew lines.
Green lines indicate skips.

6. Using the basic Fold and Sew technique, pages 22–23, dab small dots of glue in the seam allowance of the just-sewn patches. Then fold over and iron.

7. Continue to add patches until the triangle rows are completely sewn.

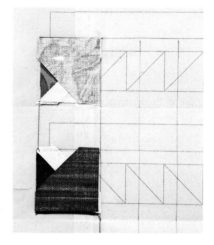

Be careful to place your third set of triangle patches so they orient correctly once they are folded over.

8. Trim the threads between the rows on both the front and back of the foundation.

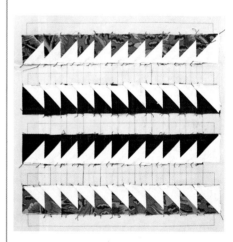

Triangle strips complete

Add Solid Strips

1. Dab glue along the entire seam allowance of a strip.

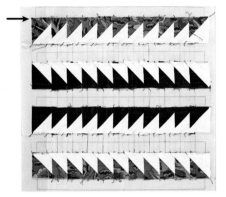

Dab glue along entire strip (green dots indicate placement).

2. Place a long fabric strip onto the pieced triangles.

3. Flip over the foundation and sew the seamline.

> ### tip
> *Sewing just a hair into the seam allowance will create sharper triangle points.*

4. Attach all of the remaining strips.

All solid strips added

5. Use the Fold and Sew technique to join the sections. (See the Joining Rows section of Fold and Sew: A Demonstration with Pyramid Triangles, pages 24–26.)

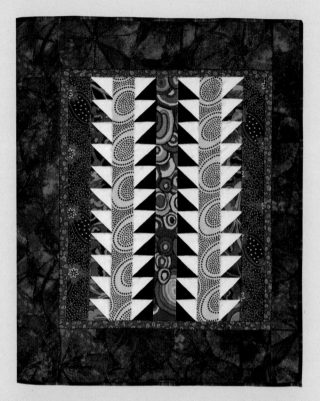

The Everlasting Tree pattern makes a great notepad cover.

For Grammy, 11″ × 12½″, Terrie Sandelin, 2007

FLYING GEESE

FINISHED FOUNDATION: 7¾″ × 10″ ◆ **TIME: 6 HOURS**

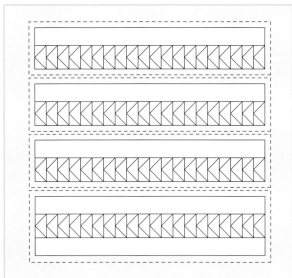

Full-size Flying Geese foundation pattern is on the pullout. Note: Foundation is rotated 90° after sewing is completed.

Dawn Flight, 13″ × 15¼″, Terrie Sandelin, quilted by Vickie Bajtelsmit, 2007

The basic construction of this quilt is the same as the Everlasting Tree foundation. The only changes are in the foundation Sew and Skip lines and in the shape, size, and placement of the patches.

Fabric Requirements

White: ¼ yard

Assorted hand-dyes in shades of orange, yellow, and purple: total of ¼ yard

Pastel peach/purple for sashing strips: ⅛ yard

Purple inner border: ⅛ yard

Peach outer border: ¼ yard

Backing: 1 fat quarter

Binding: ¼ yard

Cutting Instructions

There is no quilt layout diagram for this miniature.

Patches

You may want to add an extra ½″–1″ to each strip length for minor cutting adjustments.

Trim the half-square triangle dog ears using the ½″ Finished Half-Square Triangle patch template on the pullout or The Ruler Method: Trimming Half-Square Triangles, page 50. Trim the Flying Geese quarter-square triangles using the Flying Geese patch template on the pullout. Alternatively, you could use The Ruler Method: Trimming Flying Geese Patches, page 54, to trim the dog ears.

White triangle patches: Cut strips 1⅜″ wide for a total of 110″ in length. Crosscut into 80 squares 1⅜″ × 1⅜″; cut once on the diagonal to create 160 half-square triangles.

Pastel hand-dyes (Flying Geese): Cut strips 2¼″ wide for a total of 45″ in length. Crosscut into 20 squares 2¼″ × 2¼″; cut twice on the diagonal to create 80 quarter-square triangles.

Pastel peach/purple (sashing strips): Cut 5 strips 1¼″ × 10½″.

Purple inner border

The border measurements listed here are for straight borders. If you choose to miter your borders, add length accordingly.

Cut 2 strips ¾″ × 8¼″.

Cut 2 strips ¾″ × 11″.

Peach outer border

The border measurements listed here are for straight borders. If you choose to miter your borders, add length accordingly.

Cut 2 strips 2⅝″ × 8¾″.

Cut 2 strips 2⅝″ × 15¼″.

the ruler method:
trimming flying geese patches

Like half-square triangles, the quarter-square triangles used for the Flying Geese patches can be trimmed using a ruler rather than a template.

1. To trim the quarter-square triangle patches (cut from 2¼" squares), line up the apex of the triangle along the ¾" mark on your ruler. Align the bottom of the patch with a straight line across the ruler (which line doesn't matter). Trim off the resulting dog ear.

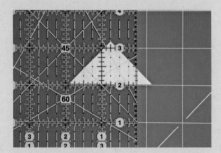

First cut

2. Spin the patch and repeat Step 1 to trim the other side.

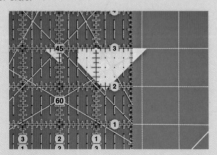

Second cut

3. Finally, align your ruler along the 1" mark of the long side of the triangle and trim off the last triangle tip.

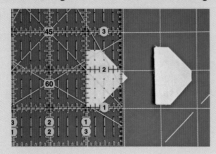

Third cut

PREPARING THE FOUNDATION

1. As with the basic Fold and Sew patterns, pages 19–21, line up adjoining seamlines that are separated by a seam allowance. Fold and crease.

2. As with the Everlasting Tree foundation, page 49, mark the horizontal and vertical seam allowance lines.

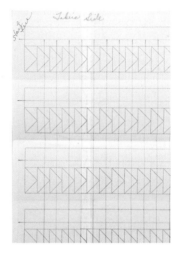

Mark horizontal and vertical seam allowance lines.

SEWING THE FOUNDATION

1. Place glue dabs on the foundation as indicated by the green dots in the photograph.

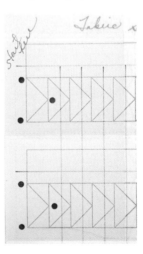

Dab glue on foundation (green dots indicate placement).

2. Place the first set of fabrics *right side up* on the foundation.

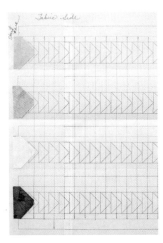

First set of patches in place

3. Dab glue onto the diagonal seam allowances of the first patch set.

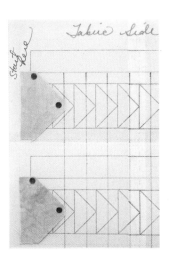

Dab glue on patches (green dots indicate placement).

4. Place the second set of patches.

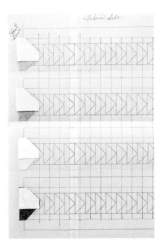

Second patch set

5. Using the Flying Geese foundation sew line diagram as a guide, sew the first seam.

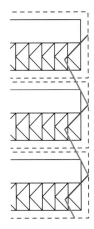

Red lines indicate sew lines.
Green lines indicate skips.

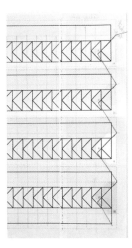

Printed side of foundation,
first seam sewn (red thread
used for demonstration purposes)

6. After all the triangle patches have been added, add the sashing strips (see Add Solid Strips, Steps 1–3, page 52). Then use the Fold and Sew technique to join the sections. (See the Joining Rows section of Fold and Sew: A Demonstration with Pyramid Triangles, pages 24–26)

BORDER FRAME

- ◆ FINISHED FOUNDATION: 10½″ × 11¼″

- ◆ FINISHED MEASUREMENT OF CENTER TOILE MOTIF WITH ¼″ FRAME: 7½″ × 8¼″

- ◆ FINISHED CENTER MOTIF: 7″ × 7¾″ (UNFINISHED 7½″ × 8¼″)

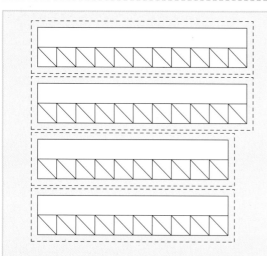

Full-size Border Frame Triangle Strips foundation patterns are on pages 58 and 59.

Birdsong, 13¾″ × 14½″, Terrie Sandelin, 2007

This is the only quilt in the book that leaves the fold out of Fold and Sew. It also has two foundations rather than one. One foundation is for the border strips and one is for the border cornerstones.

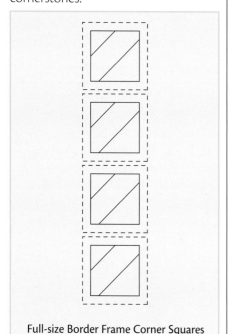

Full-size Border Frame Corner Squares foundation pattern is on page 59.

---

tip

It is easy to adjust this pattern to fit a center motif that is smaller in size: Make the inner framing border wider and/or reduce the number of triangles you finish on the foundation.

Fabric Requirements

Blue for inner border and foundation triangles: ¼ yard

Cream: ¼ yard

Brown floral for outer border and foundation triangles: ¼ yard

Backing: 1 fat quarter

Binding: ¼ yard

7½″ × 8¼″ piece for center motif

Cutting Instructions

There is no quilt layout diagram for this miniature. As you place your patches, alternate light and dark.

Triangles

You may want to add an extra ½″–1″ to each strip length for minor cutting adjustments.

Trim the half-square triangle dog ears using The Ruler Method: Trimming Half-Square Triangles, page 50, or the ¾″ Finished Half-Square Triangle patch template on the pullout.

Blue: Cut a strip 1⅝″ × 34⅛″. Crosscut into 21 squares; cut once on the diagonal to create 42 half-square triangles.

Cream: Cut a strip 1⅝″ × 34⅛″. Crosscut into 21 squares; cut once on the diagonal to create 42 half-square triangles.

Cut 2 strips 1¼″ × 8″.

Cut 2 strips 1¼″ × 8¾″.

Corner squares

You may want to add an extra ½″–1″ to each strip length for minor cutting adjustments.

Trim the 2″ squares to the correct shape using the Border Frame Corner patch template on the pullout. Trim the half-square triangle dog ears using The Ruler Method: Trimming Half-Square Triangles, page 50, or the triangle patch template indicated.

Cream: Cut a strip 2″ × 8″. Crosscut into 4 squares 2″ × 2″.

Brown floral: Cut a strip 1⅝″ × 3¼″. Crosscut into 2 squares 1⅝″ × 1⅝″; cut once on the diagonal to create 4 half-square triangles. Trim using the ¾″ Finished Half-Square Triangle patch template on the pullout.

Cut a strip 2⅛″ × 4¼″. Crosscut into 2 squares 2⅛″ × 2⅛″; cut once on the diagonal to create 4 half-square triangles. Trim using the 1¼″ Finished Half-Square Triangle patch template on the pullout.

Blue inner border (surrounding center motif)

Cut 2 strips ¾″ × 7½″.

Cut 2 strips ¾″ × 8¾″.

Brown floral outer border

Cut 2 strips 2⅛″ × 11″.

Cut 2 strips 2⅛″ × 15″.

PREPARING THE FOUNDATION

Triangle Strips

1. Because these strips are used individually and you will not be joining them, you do not need to create folds in the foundations.

2. Just as with the Everlasting Tree foundation (page 49), mark the horizontal and vertical seam allowance lines.

Corner Squares

1. You do not need to fold the foundation because each square will be used separately.

2. Mark the diagonal seam allowances.

Foundation with marked seam allowances

SEWING THE FOUNDATION

Triangle Strips

These strips are sewn in the same way as the Everlasting Tree triangle strips, page 51.

1. Place glue dabs on the foundation for the side borders.

2. Place the first set of fabrics *right side up* on the foundation.

3. Dab glue onto the diagonal seam allowances of the first patch set.

4. Place the second set of patches.

5. Using the Triangle Border foundation sew line diagram, stitch along the first foundation sew line.

6. Add the solid strips (see Add Solid Strips, Steps 1–3, page 52).

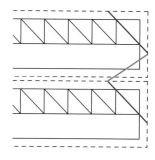

Triangle Border foundation sew line

Red lines indicate sew lines. Green lines indicate skips.

7. Continue placing patches and stitching until complete.

8. Repeat for top and bottom borders foundation.

Corner Squares

1. Place glue dabs on the foundation in the center patch seam allowances.

2. Place the first set of fabrics *right side up* on the foundation.

First set of patches in place

3. Dab glue onto the diagonal seam allowances of the first patch set.

4. Place the second set of patches.

5. Using the Border Frame Corner foundation sew line diagram, stitch along the first foundation sew line.

6. Continue placing patches and stitching until complete.

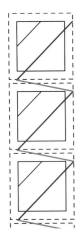

Border Frame Corner foundation sew line

Red lines indicate sew lines. Green lines indicate skips.

Fabric side of foundation, first seam sewn (red thread used for demonstration purposes)

Printed side of foundation, first seam sewn

7. After the first patch set is sewn, open the patch and press.

8. Turn the foundation 180°.

9. Repeat Steps 3–7 to sew the second set of patches.

Joining Triangle Strips and Border Squares

1. Attach the border squares to the short triangle strip lengths.

2. Attach the strips to the center toile as you would any border.

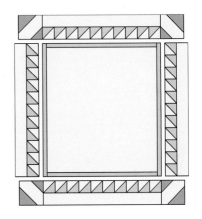

Assembly diagram

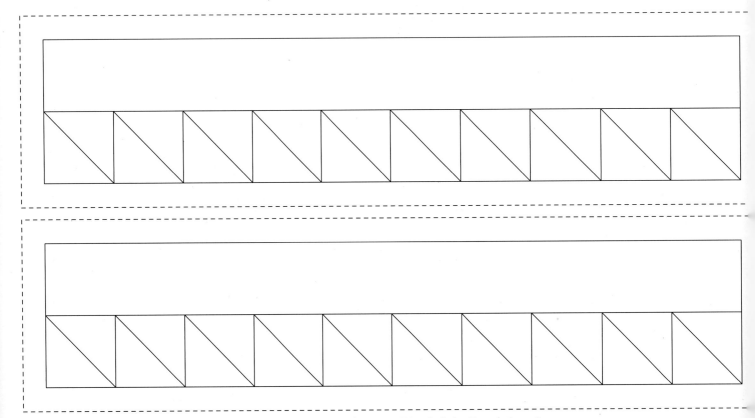

Border Frame Triangle Strips Foundation – Bottom

Border Frame Triangle Strips Foundation – Top

Border Frame Corner Foundation

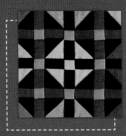

There and Back Again Projects

Just as with traditional piecing, butting seams that lie in opposing directions helps create flatter seams. The trick to this is easy: double sew the foundation. Use the Sew and Skip method to sew patches onto every other row, moving from left to right. Then pivot the foundation 180° so that what was the top is now the bottom. Then sew the remaining rows, left to right. The alternate row seams will lie in the opposite direction to your first round.

Duck and Ducklings

◆ FINISHED FOUNDATION: **7¹⁄₂″ × 7¹⁄₈″** ◆ TIME: **3** HOURS

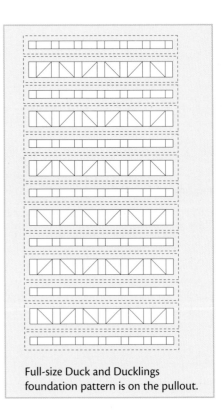

Full-size Duck and Ducklings foundation pattern is on the pullout.

Lancaster, 12″ × 12″, Terrie Sandelin, quilted by Vickie Bajtelsmit, 2007

Fabric Requirements

Black for outer border and foundation: ¼ yard

Nine assorted solids: scraps of each

Blue: ⅛ yard or scraps

Light blue: ⅛ yard or scraps

Burgundy inner border: ⅛ yard

Backing: 1 fat quarter

Binding: ¼ yard

Cutting Instructions

Letters indicate fabric placement on the quilt layout diagram for Duck and Ducklings, page 61.

Triangles

You may want to add an extra ½″–1″ to each strip length for minor cutting adjustments.

Trim the half-square triangle dog ears using The Ruler Method: Trimming Half-Square Triangles, page 50, or the ¾″ Finished Half-Square Triangle patch template on the pullout.

Black (V): Cut a strip 1⅝" × 29¼". Crosscut into 18 squares 1⅝" × 1⅝"; cut once on the diagonal to create 36 half-square triangles.

Nine solid colors (D, E, F, G, H, I, J, K, L): Cut a strip 1⅝" × 3¼" of each fabric. Crosscut each into 2 squares 1⅝" × 1⅝"; cut once on the diagonal to create 4 half-square triangles.

Rectangles

You may want to add an extra ½"–1" to each strip length for minor cutting adjustments.

Black (C): Cut a strip 1¼" × 31½". Crosscut into 36 rectangles ⅞" × 1¼".

Blue (B): Cut strips 1¼" wide for a total of 42" in length. Crosscut into 48 rectangles ⅞" × 1¼".

Squares

You may want to add an extra ½"–1" to each strip length for minor cutting adjustments.

9 solid colors (M, N, O, P, Q, R, S, T, U): Cut 1 square ⅞" × ⅞" of each fabric.

Light blue (A): Cut a strip ⅞" × 35". Crosscut into 40 squares ⅞" × ⅞".

Burgundy inner border

Cut 2 strips ¾" × 7⅝".

Cut 2 strips ¾" × 8⅛".

Black outer border

Cut 2 strips 2½" × 8⅛".

Cut 2 strips 2½" × 12⅛".

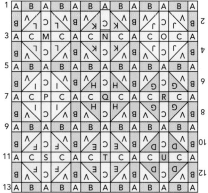

Quilt layout diagram for Duck and Ducklings foundation

Patch requirements:

Cut squares 1⅝" × 1⅝" for half-square triangles. (The number listed here is for the number of triangles. One square will yield 2 triangles.) V–36; D, E, F, G, H, I, J, K, L–4

Cut squares ⅞" × ⅞". A–40; M, N, O, P, Q, R, S, T, U–1

Cut rectangles ⅞" × 1¼". B–48, C–36

If desired, enlarge 355% to full size.

PREPARING THE FOUNDATION

1. As with the basic Fold and Sew patterns, pages 19–21, line up adjoining seamlines that are separated by a seam allowance. Fold and crease.

2. Number every *other* row on the left side of the foundation. (As always, you will mark only on the nonprinted side of the foundation.) Draw the ¼" seam allowance lines and add the lettering for these rows only, as shown in the photograph. These rows are the Pass 1 orientation of the foundation. (Note: The letters for the sashing corner squares are placed in the next patch over. If the letters were written on the patch itself, they would get covered by the previous fabric's seam allowance.)

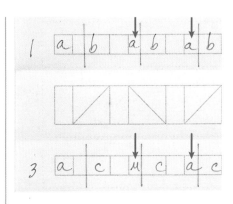

First set of alternate rows marked in blue. Arrows indicate placement of the letter for the sashing cornerstone.

3. Pivot the foundation 180° so that what was the top of your foundation is now the bottom. Number the remaining rows on the left side of the foundation for Pass 2. Draw in the red seam allowance lines and add lettering for these rows only. Shift the lettering of the ¼" rectangle patches to the next patch over. The lettering of the skipped rows will be upside down compared with the first set of rows you marked.

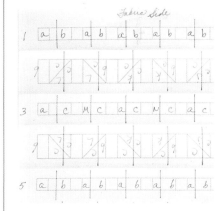

Second set of alternate rows marked in green

> ## tip
> *Using different color inks on the two alternate rows makes it easier to keep track of which is which as you sew your foundation.*

SEWING THE FOUNDATION

Odd-Numbered Rows

1. Place glue dabs on the foundation, only on the odd-numbered rows.

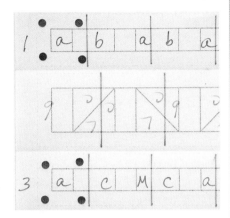

Dab glue on first set of alternate rows (green dots indicate placement).

2. Place the first patch set.

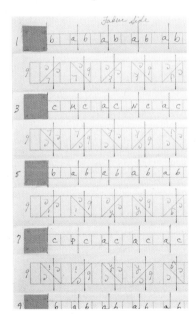

First set of patches in place

3. Place glue dabs in the right seam allowance of the first patch set and attach the second set of patches.

4. Using the Duck and Ducklings—Pass 1 foundation sew line diagram as a guide, flip over the foundation and sew the first set of patches.

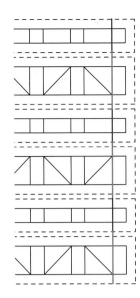

Duck and Ducklings—Pass 1 foundation sew line diagram. Red lines indicate sew lines. Green lines indicate skips.

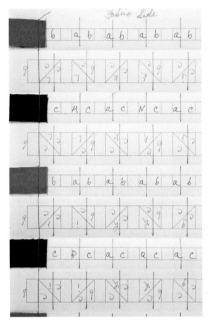

Printed side of foundation, first pass sewn (red thread used for demonstration purposes)

tip

If your sewing machine allows you to dictate needle up or needle down, choose needle up.

5. Continue to add patches until you have completed the odd-numbered rows. Trim the loose threads from both the front and back of the foundation where you skipped.

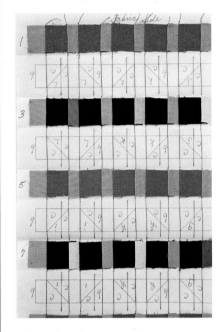

Odd-numbered rows complete

Even-Numbered Rows

1. Pivot the foundation so that what was the bottom of the foundation is now the top (Pass 2 orientation).

2. Place glue dabs on the foundation, this time on the **even-numbered rows**.

3. Place the first and second sets of patches, making sure the triangle patches are oriented correctly so they cover the patch once they are folded over.

4. Stitch using the Duck and Ducklings—Pass 2 foundation sew line diagram as a guide.

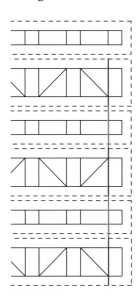

Duck and Ducklings—Pass 2 foundation sew line diagram. Red lines indicate sew lines. Green lines indicate skips.

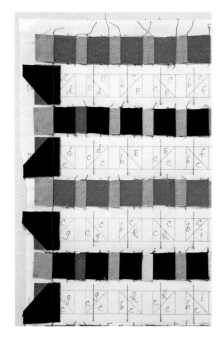

Fabric side of foundation, second pass sewn (red thread used for demonstration purposes)

5. Place glue dabs in the seam allowances.

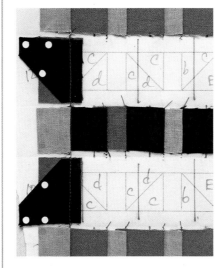

Dab glue in triangle patch seam allowances (green dots indicate placement).

6. Continue to add patches until you have completed the even-numbered rows. On both the front and the back of the foundation, trim the loose threads where you skipped.

7. Join odd- and even-numbered rows using the basic Fold and Sew technique, pages 24–25.

Additional Color Variations

How about a Halloween treat bag?

Leaf Dance, 12¼" × 12¼", Terrie Sandelin, quilted by Vickie Bajtelsmit, 2007

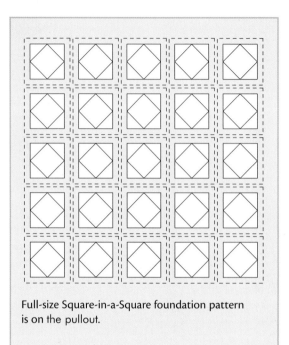

Full-size Square-in-a-Square foundation pattern is on the pullout.

Some traditional blocks, such as Courthouse Steps and Square-in-a-Square, build from the inside out. Using the Island Joins method allows you to sew these separate blocks together so you can press seams open or pivot their direction for flatter seams.

◆ square-in-a-square quilts

PREPARING THE FOUNDATION

1. As with the basic Fold and Sew patterns, pages 19–21, align adjoining seam-lines that are separated by a seam allowance. Fold and crease. Note: You will need to fold the foundation both vertically and horizontally.

2. Mark the ¼" seam allowance lines that surround the on-point squares.

3. If you are making either the Center Star or the Four Stars mini, mark the patch placement letters on the foundation. Be sure to place the letters for the triangle patches outside the seam allowance of the center square.

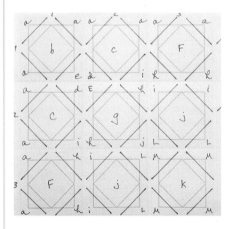

Marked Square-in-a-Square foundation

SEWING THE FOUNDATION

Blocks

1. Place glue dabs at the corners of the center squares.

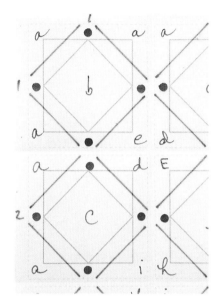

Dab glue on foundation (green dots indicate placement).

2. Place *all* the center square patches.

First set of patches in place

3. Use the Square-in-a-Square foundation sew line diagram, page 66, as a guide for the patch order. Dab glue in the seam allowance of a corner square and add the first triangle patch. After sewing, place glue dabs in the triangle seam allowance, fold over, and iron.

First triangle patch in place

4. Continue using the foundation sew line diagram as a guide as you add patches in diagonal rows until the first pass of the foundation is complete. When you skip over part of the foundation, take only a small jog over in the gap between the seam allowances.

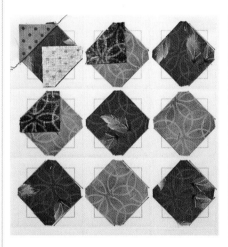

Second row of triangle patches placed and ready to sew

First pass of foundation complete

5. Pivot and sew the foundation once again, adding the remaining patches.

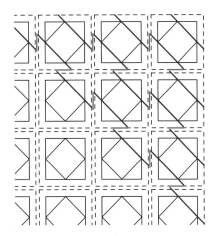

Square-in-a-Square foundation sew line diagram. Red lines indicate sew lines. Green dotted lines indicate skips.

tip

If your sewing machine allows you to dictate needle up or needle down position, choose needle up.

Second pass of foundation complete

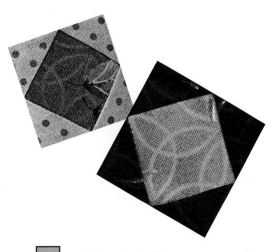

Island Joins

It is important to distinguish between interior and exterior seam allowances when joining the blocks. An exterior seam allowance surrounds the outside of the foundation. Interior seam allowance includes all those seams that are in the inside of the foundation.

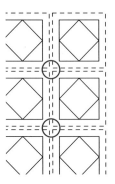

Red circles indicate interior seams.

1. Fold a row onto an adjoining row.

First fold, ready to stitch

2. As you sew your foundation, you will sew *through* the exterior seam allowance and *skip over* the interior seam allowance. Begin just beyond the outer seam allowance and sew up to the end of the first seam allowance line. Lift the needle, move the foundation, and drop the needle back in where the next seam allowance begins.

3. Continue to sew *only* on the seamlines, skipping over all of the interior seam allowances. Sew *through* the final exterior seam allowance.

Sew first folded seam.

4. Open the foundation and finger-press.

Unfold foundation and finger-press.

5. Repeat Steps 1–4 to join the remaining rows.

First set of parallel seams complete—fabric side

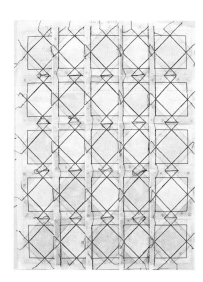

First set of parallel seams complete—foundation side

6. Clip ⅜" into the fold line of the interior seams. Be sure to clip the threads on both top and bottom. This will allow the foundation to fold over easily as you sew the remaining rows together.

Clip into fold between blocks.

7. Fold a row onto the next, right sides together.

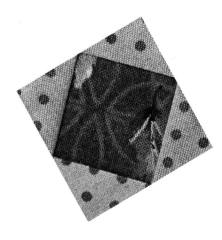

8. Stitch the seam. *As you sew along the seamline, be sure that the flaps of the seam allowance, both top and bottom, are folded out of the way of the needle.* As you approach an interior seam allowance, the flaps should be folded towards you. Stitch up to the flaps, lift the needle to skip over the interior seam allowance, fold the flaps away from you and drop the needle just past the flaps at the beginning of the next seamline. Continue to sew the remaining seamlines, always skipping over the interior seam allowances and folding the flaps out of the way of the needle. You should **never** stitch through the flaps. Remember to sew *through* the final exterior seam allowance.

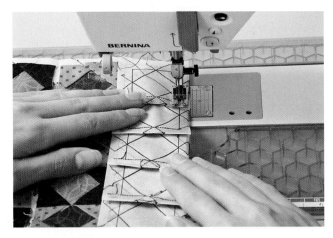

Seam allowance flaps, both top and bottom, fold forward near end of sew line.

As you skip over the seam allowance, beginning a new seamline, seam allowance flaps fold away from you.

9. Continue joining rows until the foundation is complete.

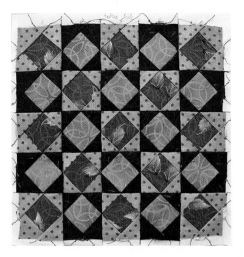

All rows joined—fabric side of foundation

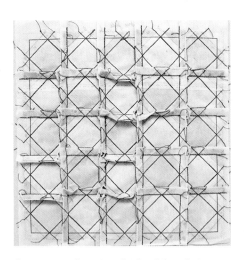

All rows joined—printed side of foundation

10. Once the foundation is completely sewn, treat it the same as any other Fold and Sew foundation: Trim the extra paper from between the seams, trim the outer seam allowances, and remove the paper. (Joining Rows, Steps 5–8, pages 25–26.)

11. Press the seams open to create a flatter quilt top.

Seams pressed open to reduce bulk

Island Joins Projects

All of the projects in this chapter are made using the Fold and Sew technique. For step-by-step directions, see Fold and Sew: A Demonstration with Pyramid Triangles, pages 19–26.

Square-in-a-Square Quilts

CENTER STAR ◆ FINISHED FOUNDATION: 7½″ × 7½″ ◆ TIME: 3 HOURS

Dargate Star, 11¾″ × 11¾″, Terrie Sandelin, 2007

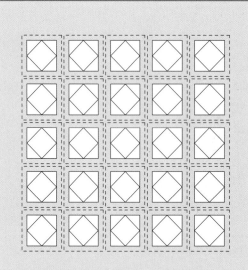

Full-size Square-in-a-Square foundation pattern is on the pullout.

Fabric Requirements

Cheddar print on cream background: ⅛ yard or scraps

Cheddar dots on cream background: ⅛ yard or scraps

Cheddar: ⅛ yard or scraps

Two medium blues: ⅛ yard or scraps of each

Dark blue: scraps

Dark blue for outer border and foundation: ¼ yard

Cheddar inner border: ⅛ yard

Backing: 1 fat quarter

Binding: ¼ yard

Cutting Instructions

Letters indicate fabric placement on the quilt layout diagram for the Square-in-a-Square—Center Star variation, page 70.

The strip width for the center squares is 1⁹⁄₁₆″. Most rulers do not have ¹⁄₁₆″ divisions. Instead, line up the fabric halfway between the ½″ and ⅝″ marks.

Center squares

You may want to add an extra ½″–1″ to each strip length for minor cutting adjustments.

Trim the tips off the corner squares using the Square-in-a-Square patch template on the pullout.

Cheddar print on cream background (N): Cut a strip 1⁹⁄₁₆″ × 6¼″. Crosscut into 4 squares 1⁹⁄₁₆″ × 1⁹⁄₁₆″.

Cheddar dots on cream background (C): Cut a strip 1⁹⁄₁₆″ × 12½″. Crosscut into 8 squares 1⁹⁄₁₆″ × 1⁹⁄₁₆″.

Dark blue (B): Cut a strip 1⁹⁄₁₆″ × 6¼″. Crosscut into 4 squares 1⁹⁄₁₆″ × 1⁹⁄₁₆″.

Dark blue (F, G, K): Cut a strip 1⁹⁄₁₆″ × 14¹⁄₁₆″. Crosscut into 9 squares 1⁹⁄₁₆″ × 1⁹⁄₁₆″.

Corner triangles

You may want to add an extra ½″–1″ to each strip length for minor cutting adjustments.

Trim the half-square triangle dog ears using The Ruler Method: Trimming Half-Square Triangles, page 50, or the ¾″ Finished Half-Square Triangle patch template on the pullout.

Cheddar print on cream background (E, J): Cut a strip 1⅝″ × 9¾″. Crosscut into 6 squares 1⅝″ × 1⅝″; cut once on the diagonal into 12 half-square triangles.

Cheddar (H, M): Cut a strip 1⅝″ × 16¼″. Crosscut into 10 squares 1⅝″ × 1⅝″; cut once on the diagonal into 20 half-square triangles.

Dark blue (L): Cut a strip 1⅝″ × 6½″. Crosscut into 4 squares 1⅝″ × 1⅝″; cut once on the diagonal into 8 half-square triangles.

Medium blue (A): Cut a strip 1⅝″ × 29¼″. Crosscut into 18 squares 1⅝″ × 1⅝″; cut once on the diagonal into 36 half-square triangles.

Medium blue (D, I): Cut a strip 1⅝″ × 19½″. Crosscut into 12 squares 1⅝″ × 1⅝″; cut once on the diagonal into 24 half-square triangles.

Cheddar inner border

Cut 2 strips ¾″ × 8″.

Cut 2 strips ¾″ × 8½″.

Blue outer border

Cut 2 strips 2⅛″ × 8½″.

Cut 2 strips 2⅛″ × 11¾″.

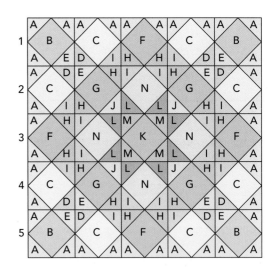

Quilt layout diagram for Square-in-a-Square foundation—Center Star variation

Patch requirements:
Cut center squares 1⁹⁄₁₆″ × 1⁹⁄₁₆″. B–4, C–8, F–4, G–4, N–4, K–1

Cut squares 1⅝″ × 1⅝″ for half-square triangles. (The number listed here is for the number of triangles. One square will yield 2 triangles.) A–36, D–8, E–8, H–16, I–16, J–4, L–8, M–4

If desired, enlarge 300% to full size.

Refer to Island Joins: A Demonstration with Square-in-a-Square, pages 64–68, for assembly instructions.

Additional Color Variations

Red Star at Night, 13″ × 13″, Paula Petterson, 2007. Isn't this pattern dramatic in red and black?

FOUR STARS

◆ **FINISHED FOUNDATION:** 7½″ × 7½″ ◆ **TIME:** 3 HOURS

Fabric Requirements

Cream: ⅛ yard or scraps

Brown print: ⅛ yard or scraps

Purple: scraps

Red-on-white print: scraps

Four red prints: scraps of each

Four blue prints: scraps of each

Four light brown prints: scraps of each

Red inner border: ⅛ yard

Brown outer border: ¼ yard

Backing: 1 fat quarter

Binding: ¼ yard

Four Stars, 12½″ × 12½″, Terrie Sandelin, quilted by Vickie Bajtelsmit, 2007

Cutting Instructions

Letters indicate fabric placement on the quilt layout diagram for the Square-in-a-Square—Four Stars variation, right.

The strip width for the center squares is 1⁹⁄₁₆″. Most rulers do not have ¹⁄₁₆″ divisions. Instead, line up the fabric halfway between the ½″ and ⅝″ marks.

Center squares

You may want to add an extra ½″–1″ to each strip length for minor cutting adjustments.

Trim the tips off the corner squares using the Square-in-a-Square patch template on the pullout.

Cream (B): Cut a strip 1⁹⁄₁₆″ × 32¹³⁄₁₆″. Crosscut into 21 squares 1⁹⁄₁₆″ × 1⁹⁄₁₆″.

Two red prints (D, E): Cut 1 square 1⁹⁄₁₆″ × 1⁹⁄₁₆″ of each fabric.

Two blue prints (C, F): Cut 1 square 1⁹⁄₁₆″ × 1⁹⁄₁₆″ of each fabric.

Corner triangles

You may want to add an extra ½″–1″ to each strip length for minor cutting adjustments.

Trim the half-square triangle dog ears using The Ruler Method: Trimming Half-Square Triangles, page 50, or the ¾″ Finished Half-Square Triangle patch template on the pullout.

Brown print (A): Cut a strip 1⅝″ × 29¼″. Crosscut into 18 squares 1⅝″ × 1⅝″; cut on the diagonal into 36 half-square triangles.

Purple (H, Q): Cut a strip 1⅝″ × 6½″. Crosscut into 4 squares 1⅝″ × 1⅝″; cut once on the diagonal into 8 half-square triangles.

Red-on-white print (K, N): Cut a strip 1⅝″ × 6½″. Crosscut into 4 squares 1⅝″ × 1⅝″; cut once on the diagonal into 8 half-square triangles.

Two red prints (G, P): Cut a strip 1⅝″ × 6½″ of each fabric. Crosscut into 4 squares 1⅝″ × 1⅝″; cut once on the diagonal into 8 half-square triangles.

Two blue prints (M, J): Cut a strip 1⅝″ × 6½″ of each fabric. Crosscut into 4 squares 1⅝″ × 1⅝″; cut once on the diagonal into 8 half-square triangles.

Four light brown prints (I, L, O, R): Cut a strip 1⅝″ × 3¼″ of each fabric. Crosscut each into 2 squares 1⅝″ × 1⅝″; cut once on the diagonal into 4 half-square triangles.

Red inner border

Cut 2 strips ¾″ × 8″.

Cut 2 strips ¾″ × 8½″.

Brown outer border

Cut 2 strips 2½″ × 8½″.

Cut 2 strips 2½″ × 12½″.

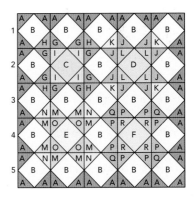

Quilt layout diagram for Square-in-a-Square foundation—Four Stars variation

Patch requirements: Cut center squares 1⁹⁄₁₆″ × 1⁹⁄₁₆″. B–21, C–1, D–1, E–1, F–1

Cut squares 1⅝″ × 1⅝″ for half-square triangles. (The number listed here is for the number of triangles. One square will yield 2 triangles.) A–36, G–8, J–8, M–8, P–8, H–4, K–4, N–4, Q–4, I–4, L–4, O–4, R–4

If desired, enlarge 415% to full size.

Refer to Island Joins: A Demonstration with Square-in-a-Square, pages 64–68, for assembly instructions.

ALTERNATING SQUARES

◆ **FINISHED FOUNDATION:** 7½″ × 7½″ ◆ **TIME:** 3 HOURS

Fabric Requirements

Gold print: ⅛ yard

Green polka dot: ⅛ yard

Burgundy: ⅛ yard

Rust leaf print for inner border and foundation: ⅛ yard

Yellow outer border: ¼ yard

Backing: 1 fat quarter

Binding: ¼ yard

Cutting Instructions

There is no quilt layout diagram for this miniature because only four fabrics are used in two alternating blocks.

The strip width for the center squares is 1⁹⁄₁₆″. Most rulers do not have ¹⁄₁₆″ divisions. Instead, line up the fabric halfway between the ½″ and ⅝″ marks.

Center squares

You may want to add an extra ½″–1″ to each strip length for minor cutting adjustments.

Trim the tips off the corner squares using the Square-in-a-Square patch template on the pullout.

Rust leaf print: Cut a strip 1⁹⁄₁₆″ × 20⁵⁄₁₆″. Crosscut into 13 squares 1⁹⁄₁₆″ × 1⁹⁄₁₆″.

Gold print: Cut a strip 1⁹⁄₁₆″ × 18¾″. Crosscut into 12 squares 1⁹⁄₁₆″ × 1⁹⁄₁₆″.

Corner triangles

You may want to add an extra ½″–1″ to each strip length for minor cutting adjustments.

Trim the half-square triangle dog ears using The Ruler Method: Trimming Half-Square Triangles, page 50, or the ¾″ Finished Half-Square Triangle patch template on the pullout.

Green polka dot: Cut a strip 1⅝″ × 42¼″. Crosscut into 26 squares 1⅝″ × 1⅝″; cut once on the diagonal to create 52 half-square triangles.

Burgundy: Cut a strip 1⅝″ × 39″. Crosscut into 24 squares 1⅝″ × 1⅝″; cut once on the diagonal to create 48 half-square triangles.

Rust inner border

Cut 2 strips ¾″ × 8″.

Cut 2 strips ¾″ × 8½″.

Yellow outer border

Cut 2 strips 2⅜″ × 8½″.

Cut 2 strips 2⅜″ × 12¼″.

Refer to Island Joins: A Demonstration with Square-in-a-Square, pages 64–68, for assembly instructions.

Leaf Dance, 12¼″ × 12¼″, Terrie Sandelin, quilted by Vickie Bajtelsmit, 2007

Additional Color Variations

Button Box, 12″ × 12″, Terrie Sandelin, 2007. The Square-in-a-Square design provides a great opportunity for displaying beads or antique buttons.

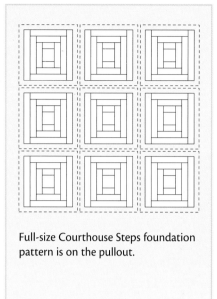

Full-size Courthouse Steps foundation pattern is on the pullout.

Blue and Brown, 11¼" × 11¼", Terrie Sandelin, 2007

Fabric Requirements

Red: scraps

Dark brown: ⅛ yard or scraps

Dark blue: scraps

Three light browns: ⅛ yard or scraps of each

Medium blue: scraps

Red-on-white print inner border: ⅛ yard

Brown floral outer border: ⅛ yard

Backing: 1 fat quarter

Binding: ¼ yard

Cutting Instructions

Shading and numbers indicate fabric placement on the quilt layout diagram for Courthouse Steps, page 74.

The strip width for the courthouse "logs" is **¹³/₁₆"**. Most rulers do not have **¹/₁₆"** divisions. Instead, line up the fabric halfway between the **³/₄"** and **⁷/₈"** marks.

Red (center squares)

You may want to add an extra ½"–1" to each strip length for minor cutting adjustments.

Cut a strip 1⅛" × 10⅛". Crosscut into 9 squares 1⅛" × 1⅛".

Corner and center blocks

You may want to add an extra ½"–1" to each strip length for minor cutting adjustments.

Dark blue: *Round 1*—Cut a strip ¹³/₁₆" × 11¼". Crosscut into 10 rectangles ¹³/₁₆" × 1⅛". *Round 2*—Cut a strip ¹³/₁₆" × 17½". Crosscut into 10 rectangles ¹³/₁₆" × 1¾".

Light brown 1: *Round 3*—Cut a strip ¹³/₁₆" × 17½". Crosscut into 10 rectangles ¹³/₁₆" × 1¾". *Round 4*—Cut a strip ¹³/₁₆" × 23¾". Crosscut into 10 rectangles ¹³/₁₆" × 2⅜".

Dark brown: *Round 5*—Cut a strip ¹³/₁₆" × 23¾". Crosscut into 10 rectangles ¹³/₁₆" × 2⅜". *Round 6*—Cut a strip ¹³/₁₆" × 30". Crosscut into 10 rectangles ¹³/₁₆" × 3".

Alternate blocks

You may want to add an extra ½"–1" to each strip length for minor cutting adjustments.

Light brown 2: *Round 1*—Cut a strip ¹³⁄₁₆" × 9". Crosscut into 8 rectangles ¹³⁄₁₆" × 1⅛". *Round 2*—Cut a strip ¹³⁄₁₆" × 14". Crosscut into 8 rectangles ¹³⁄₁₆" × 1¾".

Medium blue: *Round 3*—Cut a strip ¹³⁄₁₆" × 14". Crosscut into 8 rectangles ¹³⁄₁₆" × 1¾". *Round 4*—Cut a strip ¹³⁄₁₆" × 19". Crosscut into 8 rectangles ¹³⁄₁₆" × 2⅜".

Light brown 3: *Round 5*—Cut a strip ¹³⁄₁₆" × 19". Crosscut into 8 rectangles ¹³⁄₁₆" × 2⅜". *Round 6*—Cut a strip ¹³⁄₁₆" × 24". Crosscut into 8 rectangles ¹³⁄₁₆" × 3".

Red-on-white inner border

The border measurements listed here are for straight borders. If you choose to miter your borders, add length accordingly.

Cut 2 strips ¾" × 8".

Cut 2 strips ¾" × 8½".

Brown floral outer border

The border measurements listed here are for straight borders. If you choose to miter your borders, add length accordingly.

Cut 2 strips 1⅞" × 8½".

Cut 2 strips 1⅞" × 11¼".

Refer to Island Joins: A Demonstration with Square-in-a-Square, pages 64–68, for assembly instructions.

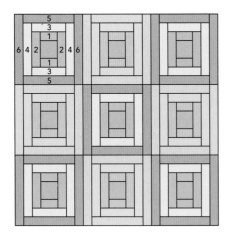

Courthouse Steps quilt layout diagram

If desired, enlarge 340% to full size.

PREPARING THE FOUNDATION

1. As with the basic Fold and Sew patterns, pages 19–21, line up adjoining seamlines that are separated by a seam allowance. Fold and crease. Note: You will need to fold the foundation both vertically and horizontally.

2. Because the "logs" on the Courthouse Steps are so narrow, colored shading is used on the quilt layout diagram rather than letters to indicate the placement of your light/dark variations. Mark X's on your foundation to help remind you where the light fabrics fall.

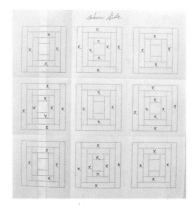

Light areas marked on creased foundation

3. The numbers on the quilt layout diagram indicate the order in which you add strips (Round 1, Round 2, etc.). Use the same numbers on your fabric guide to help you select the right strip length as you sew. This variation of Courthouse Steps has 2 blocks: Block A with a dark outer edge and Block B with a lighter outer edge.

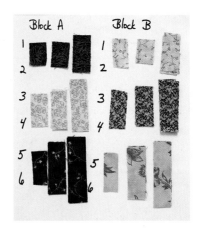

Courthouse Steps fabric guide

4. With this foundation, you will use the existing seamlines as a guide for patch placement. You do not need to draw in seam allowance lines.

SEWING THE FOUNDATION

1. Place glue dabs as illustrated by the green dots in the photograph.

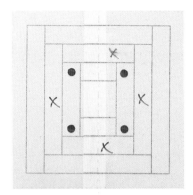

Dab glue on foundation (green dots indicate placement).

2. Set all the center square patches. Because the width of the logs is just over ¼", line up the edge of the patch just shy of the next seamline.

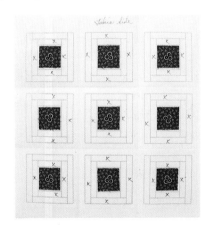

All center square patches in place

3. Use the Courthouse Steps foundation sew line diagram, right, as a guide for patch order. Dab glue in the seam allowance on the *top side only* of the center squares. Add the first set of patches.

4. Stitch the first set of patches according to the foundation sew line diagram.

5. Glue, fold over, and iron the just-sewn patches onto the foundation. Dab glue in the bottom side seam allowance of the center squares. Add the remaining first round patches.

6. On both the front and the back of the foundation, trim the loose threads from where you skipped.

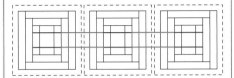

Courthouse Steps foundation sew line diagram. Red lines indicate sew lines. Green lines indicate skips.

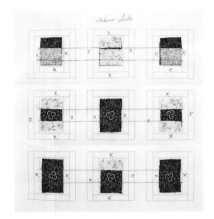

First round of patches stitched

Additional Color Variations

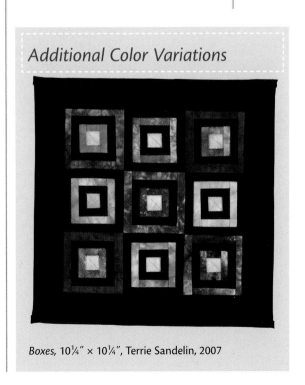

Boxes, 10¼" × 10¼", Terrie Sandelin, 2007

7. Continue to add rounds until all the blocks are complete. Remember to clip the threads, both front and back, as you add the rounds.

All blocks complete

8. Use the Island Joins method, pages 66–67 to join the blocks together.

Red and Black, 12″ × 12″, Terrie Sandelin, 2007

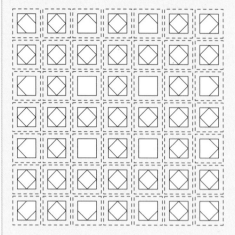

Full-size Square-in-a-Square: Nine Star foundation pattern is on the pullout.

This is the most challenging quilt in the book. I recommend that you try your hand at two or three of the simpler quilts before tackling this one!

The key difference between the Square-in-a-Square: Nine Star and your basic Square-in-a-Square foundation is that not all of the blocks on the Nine Star are full Square-in-a-Square patterns. Instead, the number of corner triangles in each block ranges from zero to four. This allows the look of a more intricate pattern without adding unnecessary seams.

You'll use the Nine Star template to cut the center square to the correct shape. Other than using the template to create different shapes, the construction method is the same as for the other Square-in-a-Square patterns. You will skip over more sections, because some squares do not need to be sewn. However, the basic pattern of sewing across the foundation on the diagonal remains the same.

For the center squares, cut a 1½″ × 1½″ square. Use the Nine Star template on the pullout, to trim to the required patch size. The Cutting Instructions state how many corners to trim.

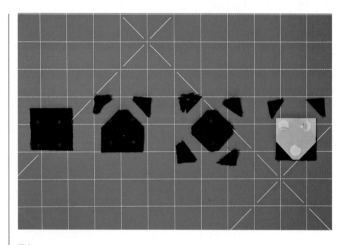

Trim corners.

tip

Before beginning this quilt, be sure to review the directions for making the basic Square-in-a-Square miniature, pages 64–69.

Fabric Requirements

Gold: ⅛ yard or scraps

Cream: ⅛ yard or scraps

Five reds: scraps of each

Five blacks: scraps of each

Tan: ⅛ yard or scraps

Black inner border: ⅛ yard

Red outer border: ¼ yard

Backing: 1 fat quarter

Binding: ¼ yard

Cutting Instructions

Letters indicate fabric placement on the quilt layout diagram for Square-in-a-Square: Nine Star, right.

Center squares

You may want to add an extra ½"–1" to each strip length for minor cutting adjustments.

Trim the tips off the center squares using the Square-in-a-Square: Nine Star template on the pullout.

Cream (B): Cut strips 1½" × a total of 60". Crosscut into 40 squares 1½" × 1½". Trim as follows:

    24 squares: Trim all 4 corners.

    4 squares: Trim 3 corners.

    8 squares: Trim 2 corners.

    4 squares: Trim 0 corners.

Five blacks (C, E, G, I, K): Cut 1 square 1½" × 1½" of each fabric. Trim all 4 corners of each square.

Four reds (D, F, H, J): Cut 1 square 1½" × 1½" of each fabric. Trim all 4 corners of each square.

Corner triangles

You may want to add an extra ½"–1" to each strip length for minor cutting adjustments.

Trim the half-square triangle dog ears using The Ruler Method: Trimming Half-Square Triangles, page 50, or the ½" Finished Half-Square Triangle patch template on the pullout.

Gold (A): Cut a strip 1⅜" × 35¾". Crosscut into 26 squares 1⅜" × 1⅜"; cut once on the diagonal to create 52 half-square triangles.

Five reds (L, N, P, R, T): Cut a strip 1⅜" × 5½" of each fabric. Crosscut each into 4 squares 1⅜" × 1⅜"; cut once on the diagonal to create 8 half-square triangles.

Four blacks (M, O, Q, S): Cut a strip 1⅜" × 5½" of each fabric. Crosscut each into 4 squares 1⅜" × 1⅜"; cut once on the diagonal to create 8 half-square triangles.

Tan (U, V, W, X, Y, Z, AB, AC, AD): Cut a strip 1⅜" × 24¾". Crosscut into 18 squares 1⅜" × 1⅜"; cut once on the diagonal to create 36 half-square triangles.

Black inner border

Cut 2 strips ¾" × 7½".

Cut 2 strips ¾" × 8".

Red outer border

Cut 2 strips 2½" × 8".

Cut 2 strips 2½" × 12".

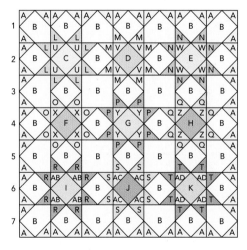

Quilt layout diagram for Square-in-a-Square: Nine Star foundation

Patch requirements:

Cut center squares 1½" × 1½". B–40; C, D, E, F, G, H, I, J, K–1

Cut squares 1⅜" × 1⅜" for half-square triangles. (The number listed here is for the number of triangles. One square will yield 2 triangles.) A–52; L, M, N, O, P, Q, R, S, T–8; U, V, W, X, Y, Z, AB, AC, AD–4

If desired, enlarge 295% to full size.

PREPARING THE FOUNDATION

1. Line up adjoining seamlines. Fold and crease. Note: You will need to fold the foundation both vertically and horizontally.

2. Mark the ¼" seam allowance lines that surround the on-point squares.

3. Mark the patch placement letters onto the foundation. Be sure to place the letters for the triangle patches outside the seam allowance of the center square.

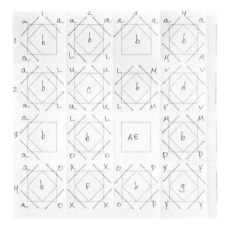

Place letters outside seam allowances of center squares.

SEWING THE FOUNDATION

1. Place glue dots on the foundation as shown. Because the patch shapes vary from square to square, glue placement will vary; place the dabs wherever the corners of the fabric lie.

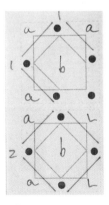

Dab glue on foundation (green dots indicate placement).

2. Place *all* the center square patches.

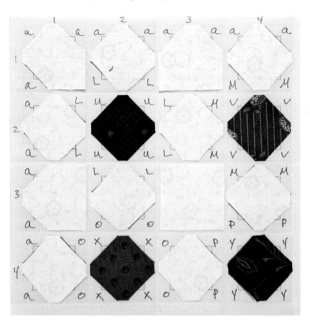

First set of patches in place

3. Use the Square-in-a-Square: Nine Star foundation sew line diagram as a guide for patch order. Place and sew the first set of patches. Notice how the sew lines on this foundation skip over squares with unpieced corners.

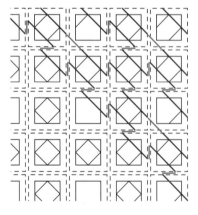

Square-in-a-Square: Nine Star foundation sew line diagram. Red lines indicate sew lines. Green lines indicate skips.

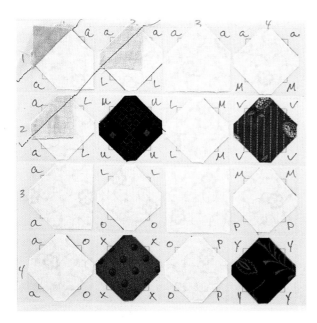

Adding triangle patches—fabric side (red thread used for demonstration purposes)

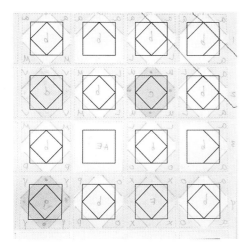

Adding triangle patches—foundation side

4. When the first patch set is complete, add the second set of patches to complete the foundation.

5. Stitch Island Joins just as you would for regular Square-in-a-Square foundations, pages 66–67.

Resources

For a list of other fine books from C&T Publishing, ask for a free catalog:

C&T Publishing, Inc.

P. O. Box 1456

Lafayette, CA 94549

(800) 284-1114

Email: ctinfo@ctpub.com

Website: www.ctpub.com

C&T Publishing's professional photography services are now available to the public.

Visit us at www.ctmediaservices.com.

For quilting supplies:

Cotton Patch

1025 Brown Avenue

Lafayette, CA 94549

Store: (925) 284-1177

Mail order: (925) 283-7883

Email: CottonPa@aol.com

Website: www.quiltusa.com

Note: Fabrics used in the quilts shown may not be currently available, as fabric manufacturers keep most fabrics in print for only a short time.

The Electric Quilt Company

www.electricquilt.com

ReproductionFabrics.com

A wonderful source for beautiful reproduction fabrics

Roxanne International

Roxanne Glue-Baste-It

www.thatperfectstitch.com

Photo by Jonas Sandelin, Terrie's son

About the Author

Terrie made her first quilts 30 years ago for her two sons and nephew. Back then, quilting information was so scarce, she didn't even know there *was* such a thing as a quilting hoop. After that, there was a long hiatus from quilting while she went back to school and raised her children. When she returned to quilting years later, it was with real delight that she discovered a sudden wealth of information about all things quilting—a golden age, indeed. Since then, there's been no looking back. She lives in Colorado with her husband and teaches literature (another passion) at Colorado State University.